Deep Memory, Exuberant Hope

Deep Memory, Exuberant Hope

Contested Truth in a Post-Christian World

WALTER BRUEGGEMANN

edited by Patrick D. Miller

FORTRESS PRESS

Minneapolis

Library of Congress Cataloging-in-Publication Data

Brueggemann, Walter.
    Deep memory, exuberant hope : contested truth in a post-Christian world /
Walter Brueggemann ; edited by Patrick D. Miller.
        p. cm.
    Includes bibliographical references and indexes.
    ISBN 0-8006-3237-0 (alk. paper)
    1. Bible. O.T. —Theology. I. Miller, Patrick D. II. Title.

BS1192.5 .B775 2000
230'.0411—dc21   00-024752

Manufactured in the U.S.A.   AF 1-3237
04   03   02   01   2   3   4   5   6   7   8   9   10

Contents

Editor's Foreword

THIS VOLUME IS THE THIRD IN A SERIES OF WALTER BRUEGGEMANN'S biblical and theological essays. The careful reader will have noted a similar cover on each of the volumes, marking them as a series. The first book, *The Covenanted Self* (1999), deals with covenant and the commandments and their significance for human existence. The second, *Texts That Linger, Words That Explode* (2000), takes up a part of the biblical corpus that has been to the forefront of Brueggemann's writing and speaking for many years: the prophets. Now in this last of the series, a further dimension of Brueggemann's work comes to the fore in a collection of essays whose primary focus is upon *speech* and *rhetoric*.

In a unique way, Brueggemann combines a passionate awareness of the nature and character of speech in Scripture with a demonstrated skill in rhetoric that permeates his own writing and speaking. That is, while focusing upon rhetoric and the power of language, he demonstrates both in all his writing as well as in his lecturing. There are few if any major lectureships in the field of biblical studies in this country to which he has not been invited. But his interest and skill in speech and rhetoric is well evidenced by the number of times he has been invited to lecture on preaching, for example, at the Academy of Homiletics meetings or the Lyman Beecher Lectures on Preaching at Yale (*Finally Comes the Poet*, 1989). Those who hear him learn by his teaching and his example that the medium really is the message, that communication with power—divine and human—persuades the hearers of the truthfulness of the word that is conveyed and that the form of communication participates significantly with the material to produce the whole word of truth. And I know no one who teaches better by the way he answers questions from his listeners than does Walter Brueggemann.

This deep concern for communication of Scripture and its meaning is reflected in the essays in this volume in a very forthright way. In these pages, Brueggemann turns directly to his largest audience, pastors of congregations who week by week take up the word to preach it faithfully and who regularly find that this Old Testament scholar brings it to life for them and does so in ways that signal what it can mean to those disparate folk who sit in their sanctuaries on Sunday mornings. His slant is not typical of books on preaching. There is little optimism and no triumphalism about preaching. It is a demanding and difficult task, and Brueggemann's intention is not to provide homiletical helps—though such are never to be scorned (as any preacher knows well)—but to suggest a style of preaching, a style that is more substance and stance than it is technique. His lack of optimism concerns the situation in which preaching takes place, about the world we live in and the tenor of our times; but he knows the power of the gospel, and those who sit at his feet find their own convictions about that power renewed and their preaching invigorated.

For Brueggemann, however, the speech act of Christian belief, the rhetorical activity of communicating the word of God, is not confined to the pulpit but happens in the acts of listening to the Scriptures taught and interpreted and in the reading of them. His well-known popularity as a lecturer is a manifestation of the power of his words and the rhetorical skill with which he draws in listeners and readers to hear hard words and see hopeful visions. He is unflinching in tackling the disturbing dimensions of our cultural life, such as consumerism and greed, militarism and violence, and he refuses to accept the often assumed dichotomy between piety and justice. The community of faith is in the foreground in his writing and in his speaking. The power of the Scriptures to speak truth to power and comfort to the comfortless is a prominent dimension of most of his writing.

In this final section, the power of rhetoric arises often out of the interpretation of the prophets, more specifically and frequently one of those prophets who has caught Brueggemann's mind and heart, the unknown prophet of the exile whom we dub Second Isaiah. Brueggemann himself would never be presumptuous enough to align himself with those earlier prophetic voices, but their ancient texts do indeed explode with power afresh in his own gift of prophetic speech. His own power of communication turns his lectures/essays into genuine speech acts that accomplish in their hearers a responsive reaction. Careful readers (and listeners) will observe at least three ways in which Brueggemann accomplishes this. One is in his frequent *use of words as identifiable signs of his own idiom*, for example, "odd," "daring," "subversive," "Saturday," "disputatious," and the like—all of which are common and loaded words in his rhetoric, expressing a sense about biblical literature that is Brueggemann's own angle of vision but one that makes sense to those who encounter it. A second medium of proclamation is his love of *dialectical rhetoric*, for example, the "certitude of autonomy and the certitude of absolutism" or "fearful conformity and troubled autonomy" or "the liturgy of abundance and the myth of scarcity." Finally his *emphatic syntax* expressed in accented speech and italicized words forces the listener/reader to sit up and pay attention. These words matter!

There is one further contribution of these essays that will interest many readers. In various ways, they lay the groundwork for Brueggemann's magisterial *Theology of the Old Testament*. At least two are especially evident and worth mentioning:

1) Here the reader will encounter Brueggemann's development of the

image of the courtroom and of the Old Testament as various forms of *testimony*, a way of approaching the Scriptures that points to the centrality of rhetoric and speech and suggests the character of the Bible as requiring decision. At this point, Brueggemann makes a risky move that some have criticized severely. He has ventured to set aside ontological claims—not to deny them, which has been a common misreading of his work—arguing that the community of faith has access to the God who speaks and acts in Scripture only through the testimony that is found there. In a sense, Brueggemann bypasses the usual historical criteria for the truthfulness of the text in order to claim that the reality of which the Bible speaks arises out of the testimony. He speaks of "the constitutive power of speech" and argues that "those who value rhetoric in a central way recognize that speech constitutes reality in some decisive way" ("Texts that Linger, Not Yet Overcome"). In the problem that arose out of Gerhard von Rad's work as to whether what matters is Israel's testimony or some historical reality behind it, Brueggemann has cut the Gordian knot by arguing that the testimony is the reality. In the postmodern context, he suggests that the various voices of God-speech in the Scriptures "are all advocates in the debate about how to voice provisional identity of the undoubted unaccommodating Other" ("The Role of Old Testament Theology in Old Testament Interpretation"). Those who read this theologian carefully will understand that every word in that quotation is weighty: his claim that the voices of Scripture are in a debate (the courtroom), that they are advocates of a point of view, that "voice" or speech is all we have from them, that the Other is unaccommodating, and that the Other is undoubted. This last adjective reminds us that however provisional the testimony, the one who is identified is truly there, not in some mode of being, but here with us, for us, against us, far from us.

At the heart of Brueggemann's *Theology* is a claim that the testimony centers in speech about Yahweh of Israel. He dares to identify the "most characteristic speech about God" ("Crisis-Evoked, Crisis-Resolving Speech"). Finding that speech evoked especially in crisis, Brueggemann often focuses upon the experience of exile and the modes of speech that arose from that experience (for example, "Four Indispensable Conversations Among Exiles"). In Israel's testimony, Yahweh comes to life and gives life (Ezekiel 36) to a community that has chosen death rather than life (Deut. 30:15; Jer. 8:3). The articulation of this life-giving word in a death-dealing situation is a fundamental enterprise in which Brueggemann is fully engaged in his work. Along the way, he listens well to the voices of pain that cry out to the living God in the face of death, including those who find only an abandoning absence of God ("Texts That Linger, Not Yet Overcome"). That, Brueggemann reminds us, is as much a part of the testimony as the proclamations of the good news of God's presence and activity to help.

As this second series of Brueggemann's collected essays comes to a close, the contribution of this theologian-exegete to the church's understanding of the Old Testament and of the God who speaks through it is clear. In this generation, there is no stronger or clearer spokesperson for the testimony of Israel as a word to the community of faith. The passage of time will make future readers aware of how these essays, like all writing, are observably reflective of the times and the spirit of the times in which they were written. But it will not diminish their capacity to help believers—both those of large faith and those who just barely hang on—to grasp its truthfulness and its power for their own lives and worlds.

Patrick D. Miller

Preface

IT STRIKES ME AS ODD THAT AFTER LONG YEARS OF TEACHING THE BIBLE I should now accent "a turn to the text." Especially since I have from the outset of my teaching responsibilities turned to the text, not only out of professional obligation, but also out of deep conviction. Given those many years of such a "turn," it strikes me acutely that the church in U.S. society must indeed "turn to the text," especially after mainline churches have expressly made a "turn to the subject." George Lindbeck in his influential book of 1984, *The Nature of Doctrine*, with his accent on "cultural-linguistic" urgings prepared the categories for such a turn. When undertaken from an exegetical rather than from a doctrinal perspective, however, turning the turn to the text is much more concrete and text-specific than Lindbeck's program; it is a perspective that pays attention to specific cadences, forms, nuances, and rhythms of the text. The essays offered here represent some of my recent thinking and work concerning the place and role of the biblical text in the faith and ministry of the church.

In my recent work, I have sought to be as deeply and consistently antifoundational as I am able to be. That, of course, means a resistance to any appeal to universal warrants beyond the specificities of the text. Such a perspective is closely congruent with Karl Barth's well-known phrasing, "The strange new world of the Bible." The turn to the text in contemporary church life is urgent, in my judgment, precisely because the humanness of our society from a faith perspective depends precisely upon this deep strangeness and this surprising newness that stand outside the narratives and ideologies that now govern most of our public life. It seems exactly correct to say that it is this "outsider" claims of the text that refuse accommodation or domestication that may make a difference among us, an outsider status that freshly situates the church in society. In these essays, with reference to preaching, to church polity, to economic life and much else, the text offers a fresh invitation to healthy life in the world.

Such a turn to the text means that the local congregation is an arena that pays attention to the text in all of its "thickness." This term, of course from Clifford Geertz, means that the text cannot be read at a glance, cannot be exhausted by critical methods, cannot be summed up in familiar content. The thickness requires many readings, many hearings, many interpretations, and many acts of faithful imagination, each of which may be received and heard as "a live word." To receive such a live word, the church and its interpreters must hear every nuance and go deep into memory. Such attentive remembering, however, is more than a recall of the past. It spills into the present as a neighborly ethic that contradicts selfish violence, and into the future as hope that contradicts despair. Our society is indeed increasingly thinned of memory, ethics, and hope. The biblical text offers a powerful alternative to that thinness, a thickness laden with courage, freedom, and energy.

It remains for me to thank yet again the special people who have turned my turning into a book. At Fortress Press, this is especially K. C. Hanson and Ann Delgehausen. Beyond this, Patrick Miller has invested his good judgment on my behalf and has offered welcome guidance to me in the formation of the volume. Tim Simpson has used his great care yet again in preparing indexes, and Tempie Alexander, to whom I turn as often as I turn to the text, has yet again worked her magic to transform humble offerings into workable articulation. The text has its own life; but my turning to it is in, with, and under these endlessly grace-filled people in my life. These people, especially Patrick Miller, Tim Simpson, and Tempie Alexander, have come to betoken for me the great host of people who evoke my work and engage with it, to whom I am endlessly thankful.

Walter Brueggemann
Lent 2000

1

Preaching as Sub-Version

THERE WAS A TIME, PERHAPS 250 YEARS AGO, WHEN THE CHRISTIAN preacher could count on the shared premises of the listening community, reflective of a large theological consensus. There was a time, a very long time, when the *assumption of God* completely dominated Western imagination, and the holy catholic church roughly uttered the shared consensus of all parties. That shared consensus was rough and perhaps not very healthy, but at least the preacher could work from it.

In that ancient world—moving to the modern—the consensus, deep and broad, made it all but impossible to be an atheist. Not only was the thought of a-theism intellectually not available, but emotionally and culturally there was no receptive context for such a notion. Indeed, Michael Buckley has traced the intellectual developments of the seventeenth and eighteenth centuries that made a-theism a credible intellectual alternative for the first time, and then an emotionally and culturally bearable interpretive posture.[1] As time has gone on, through the nineteenth century, citizens of the Western world have had to make a series of adjustments and settlements, seemingly unending adjustments and settlements, always at the expense of theism and in concessions to a-theism. Those concessions have been required primarily because of the emergence of a thinking autonomy in the world, rooted in Descartes and expressed belatedly in Robert Bellah's report on "Sheilaism."[2] By the time of the twentieth century, the settlement largely had been that God is still a cherished affirmation in private matters ("family values"), but the public realm is largely a-theistic, without God, so that "might makes right." Appeal is characteristically made to legitimation other than God, appeal to a public God having become increasingly difficult and embarrassing.

And now, so it seems to me, by the time of the twenty-first century, the intellectual-emotional-cultural situation of the seventeenth century, for complex reasons, has been completely reversed. A-theism is now a credible, perhaps a consensus, option for what is serious in life, and the articulation of life-with-God has become a risky intellectual outpost, perhaps as difficult and as odd and as embarrassing as was a-theism in the seventeenth century. It seems to me not so important to review all of the complex reasons for that inversion—reasons that include the rise of scientific thinking, the emergence of Enlightenment autonomy, and the shift into high-gear technology as the way to better our life, high-gear technology that begins in Research and Development and that ends, inevitably I believe, in militarism. It is more important to recognize our fairly recently changed intellectual-emotional-theological situation in which we do our preaching and, for that matter, in which we do what we can of our own trusting and believing.

1

In the seventeenth century, it was hard, courageous work to imagine—consequently reimagine—the world *without* God. And now, into the twenty-first century, in the face of Enlightenment autonomy issuing in autonomous power and autonomous knowledge, it is hard, courageous work to imagine—consequently reimagine—the world *with* God.

Of course, you understand I am speaking with evangelical particularity. I have used the terms "a-theism" and "theism" for purposes of symmetry. But you will understand that I do not in fact mean "theism," for theism of sorts is alive and well in our postmodern world. Indeed, the polls show that, in its indeterminate forms, almost everybody believes in God. But I mean, as you would expect, the peculiar trinitarian claims for God concerning the one we confess in the history of Israel and in the narrative of Jesus. Theism of certain kinds is still culturally credible, but we are speaking of none other than the creator of heaven and earth whose quintessential intention showed up, we confess, in the absence of Good Friday.

And so I pursue with you the single point. In a culture that has learned well how to imagine—how to make sense—of the world without reference to the God of the Bible, it is the preacher's primal responsibility to invite and empower and equip the community to reimagine the world as though Yahweh were a key and decisive player. The task is as upstream as was seventeenth-century a-theism. This is an uncommonly difficult intellectual task, almost sure to be misunderstood. Its difficulty is compounded, moreover, by its inescapable economic by-product, because the God of the Bible is endlessly restless with socioeconomic power arrangements that the world takes as normal. If you are like me, you keep hoping Sunday by Sunday, as we do our hard intellectual work, that folks will not immediately notice the inescapable economic implications that come with it.

I recently gave some lectures at Baldwin-Wallace College. The lectures were endowed by a very generous family that is concerned that religion should be prominent in the life of the college. Two sons of the original donor, enterprising, gracious businessmen, attended the lecture in which I did a biblical critique of capitalism. The task was not easy. It turned out all right, however, because all that was noticed by the appreciative donors was that I had quoted lots of the Bible. The rest was happily lost on them. I understand the moment of preaching, in the designated place of preaching, to be a *freeing and primitive act* that flies in the face of all our accepted certitudes, conservative and liberal.

II

I speak to you as an Old Testament teacher, though I think it is not significantly different in the New Testament. The preacher has some considerable
resources for this dangerous problematic task of reimagining the world
with Yahweh as its key player. There is the deep faith of the present community that matters more than I think we usually credit. There is the long
history of the church, written in creeds and manifestoes and architecture,
and set deep in the lives of saints who in their dangerous innocence made
this primitive faith claim unavoidable.

But mainly, in the midst of these evidences and testimonies, what the
preacher has is this old text, so remote, so difficult, so misleading, so problematic, so unintimidated. It is the enduring sound of a thousand unclear
witnesses offering a cacophony of truthfulness, the script for our own dangerous, primitive reimagining.

Of all that could be said of this script, my initial point is a simple but
crucial one. It is in *Hebrew*, not Latin. I do not say that to suggest that one
cannot read it without knowledge of Hebrew grammar, though such
knowledge is a good idea and a real advantage. I say it rather to make the
point that this text, in its very utterance, in its ways of putting things, is
completely unfamiliar to us.[3] The utterance of the primitive God of Scripture is an utterance that is in an unfamiliar mode. Let me say what I mean.

Hebrew, even for those who know it much better than do I, is endlessly
imprecise and unclear. It lacks the connecting words; it denotes rather than
connotes; it points and opens and suggests, but it does not conclude or define.
That means it is a wondrous vehicle for what is suggested but hidden, what is
filled with imprecision and inference and innuendo, a vehicle for contradiction, hyperbole, incongruity, disputation. Now the reason this may be important is that in a society of technological control and precision, we are seduced
into thinking that if we know the codes, we can pin down all meaning, get all
mysteries right and have our own way, without surprise, without deception,
without amazement, without gift, without miracle, without address, without
absence, without anything that signals mystery or risk. In such a society as
that, the church and its preachers practice another mode of speech, so that the
way we imagine is congruent with *who it is that we imagine.*[4]

Long before our contemporary technology, the church tried the same
trick with Latin; one does not need to know much Latin to know that it is
regular, precise, and symmetrical. It goes from one margin of the page to
the other; it admits of only controllable cadences. For those of us who left
the Latin liturgy in the sixteenth century, our alternative strategy has been
historical criticism, another "Latin-like" attempt to control and reduce
and tame and understand and reduce and control and reduce.

But testimony to the God of Israel known in Jesus Christ is not "Latin-
like," and it is not historical criticism–like. It is more like depth psychology,

for Freud was, in his larger discernments, thoroughly Jewish.[5] Freud understood that in dreams, in the unconscious, in the hiddenness of utterance, there are *endless zones of contradiction* that we keep negotiating—occasionally with Freudian slips—and there are *endless layers of interpretation,* no one of which can ever be more than provisional. And the reason depth psychology is marked as "depth" is that one can always push deeper into another layer of hiddenness and there find yet another disclosure of significance.

The preacher has on her hands a Subject who is not obvious and a mode of speech that is endlessly open and demanding . . . that makes preaching deeply demanding in a congregation schooled in one-dimensional, technological certitude. The offer of such technological certitude, however, not only misreads the text and the God of the text; it seriously distorts and misrepresents the true human scene, as every pastor knows, for the human scene is one of endless zones of contradiction and endless layers of interpretation, no one of which can ever be more than provisional. I suggest, for that reason, that faithful speech about God is sure to be faithful speech about the complicatedness of being human, and this in a society determined to oversimplify. I summarize the problematic of the Bible about God in this way:

1. The God of the Bible is endlessly *irascible*—capable of coming and going, judging and forgiving, speaking and remaining silent—in ways that make the next time endlessly uncertain. I do not want to overstate the case. But it is this quality that pushes the psalmists to the extremity of their imaginations, and it is this quality that evokes in the prophets daring images and affronting metaphors, because no easy language will ever get this God said right.[6]

2. The testimony we have concerning this God is *endlessly elusive.* Sometimes there is a direct offer of God, but more often there is fantasy, sideways figures, and odd articulations, some of which are covered over by church cliché, some of which are lost in the caution of translators.

3. The *irascible* character of God and the *elusive* rhetoric of the text mean that the outcome of textual testimony is deeply *polyvalent,* that is, it speaks with many voices and is profoundly open to rich variation in rendering.

The preacher stands up to make utterance about this odd, problematic God in a society that is flattened in a-theism, and has on her hands a quality of the *irascible,* the *elusive,* and the *polyvalent.* Almost none of this, moreover, is available to or recognized among most of our listeners. Because it is too unsettling and difficult, we tend to fall back on more familiar ground of safe practices, blessed ideologies, scholastic closures, or liberal crusades. Don't we all!

But the God of Israel, belatedly bodied in Jesus of Nazareth, is our Subject. Such utterance is unsettling, open, freeing, demanding. Such utterance in our time, as in all the times of our mothers and fathers, generates possibilities—public and personal—that are not otherwise possible, not otherwise doable or thinkable. When this God is uttered, the closed world of a-theism is shattered; those who hear dream dreams and see visions, sense power and receive courage, take up energy for newness where none seems offered. It is a lot to expect from an utterance, taken off from an old non-Latin subject. But it is what our mothers and father have long counted on. It is, moreover, more or less what people hope for, even in our great fear that it might come to pass.

III

My thesis is that preaching is a *sub-version*. You will recognize the play that I intend. Preaching is never dominant version, never has been. It is always a sub-version, always a version, a rendering of reality that lives under the dominant version. We may adopt a strategy of making our "under-version" sound closely like the dominant version, or an alternative strategy of show-ing our "under-version" to be in deep tension with the dominant version.

The *dominant version* of reality each of us would mark differently, but we likely would not disagree much on its nature. Perhaps the logo of the dominant version is *swoosh,* Nike, "life is for winners" of a private, indi-vidualized kind who can make it in the market or in the sports arena, who live well, are self-indulgent but who never get involved in anything outside of their own success. The Nike version of reality, deeply rooted in Western Enlightenment consumerism and in U.S. democratic capitalism, has an old history. In the Old Testament it appears as coercive Babylonian imperial expectations looking back to Egyptian brick quotas. In the New Testament it is the endless requirements of Jewish punctiliousness or the demand of Roman emperor worship; it is Luther's "works," and in our day perhaps it is "the end of welfare as we know it," the pressure to get kids into the right preschools for the sake of someday working for Intel. It is an act of domi-nant imagination that screens out all "neighbors," neighbors who can be screened out if the God of all Neighborliness can be refashioned into a God who celebrates the virtues of private achievement. It is dominant, so domi-nant, that is it taken as a given, so dominant that it sustains both liberal and conservative ideology, so dominant that even we who critique are deeply committed to it, so dominant it is not worth criticizing—too costly.

And then we preachers are summoned to get up and utter a *sub-version* of reality, an alternative version of reality that says another way of life in the world is not only possible but is peculiarly mandated and peculiarly valid. It is a *sub-version* because we must fly low, stay under the radar, and hope not to be detected too soon, a sub-version, because it does indeed intend to *sub-vert* the dominant version and to empower a community of *sub-versives* who are determined to practice their lives according to a dif-ferent way of imagining.

I understand then that preaching is a peculiar, freighted, risky act each time we do it: entrusted with an irascible, elusive, polyvalent Subject and flying low under the dominant version with a *subversive* offer of *another version* to be embraced by *subversives*.

I focus this strange act precisely on one pivot point that is fairly obvious as illustrative. The *dominant version* of reality among us is a narrative of *violence*. This can run all the way from sexual abuse and racial abuse to the strategy of wholesale imprisonment of "deviants" to military macho that passes for policy. It eventuates in road rage and in endless TV violence piped in our homes for our watching pleasure. I suspect that underlying all of these modes of violence is the *economic violence* embedded in free-market ideology, which denies an obligation of openness to the neighbor who is in truth a deep inconvenience and a drain upon resources.

If we take that as the Dominant Version, then the preacher is to sub-vert by an act of sustained imagination that is an antidote to a culture of violence and this in the name of the God whose own history is marked on numerous occasions by acts of violence. I suggest an easy identification of three dimensions of violence and three antidotal responses:

1. The taproot of violence is *material deprivation,* fostered by a myth of scarcity, the driving power of market ideology. The counter to material deprivation is a practice of sharing that is rooted in and appeals to *an affirmation of abundance.* That affirmation of abundance, rooted in the generosity of God, is deeply subversive to the deep social myth of scarcity.[7] The preacher has available the memories of that time we were in the wilderness and bread inexplicably came down from heaven, and "nobody had too little and nobody had too much" (Exod. 16:18, my paraphrase). And we have that memory of Jesus with compassion on the crowd; he took, he blessed, he broke, he gave . . . he fed five thousand people with twelve baskets of bread left over (Mark 6:30-44), and then two chapters later he did it all over again: he took, he blessed, he broke, he gave . . . he fed four thousand people with seven baskets left over (Mark 8:1-9). And then he said to his bewildered disciples: "You don't get it, do you?" (Mark 8:21, my paraphrase). When the gospel is trusted, loaves abound! And violence from common deprivation becomes obsolete.

2. The taproot of violence is *a breakdown of connections,* the severing of elemental social relationships so that folk are driven into isolation and then made desperate and frantic. I commend to you a book by Fox Butterfield, *All God's Children,* a five-generation family history that begins in the legendary violence of South Carolina in slavery and culminates in black urban crime in New York City, driven by black urban rage.[8] The focus is on the fifth generation—Willie—who is now in a New York prison, the most violent criminal ever held in that state system.

The argument of the book is that the failure to sustain a human, familial, communal social fabric, a failure rooted in the intrinsic violence of slavery, makes the strategy of violence inevitable. Of course it is easy to spot violence among poor blacks. It is the same violence, is it not, working by and among the white urban elites who know nothing but self-indulgence at the expense of the neighbor, and so the entire social fabric is reduced to a violent contest to see who can have the most and who can have first and who can have best, called "opportunity" by free-market violence wanting to escape regulation. It's not about playing well, it's about winning.

I understand none of this is a proper theme for preaching—except that since the violence of Pharaoh against the slaves, the God of Sinai has offered an alternative and an antidote to violence, an offer of covenant, a vision, a structure, and a practice that binds the "haves" and the "have-nots" into one shared community, so that we are indeed members of each other. We live in a world of kinship, where when one suffers all suffer and when one rejoices all rejoice together. It is indeed covenantal community that is the only available alternative to the dissociation that fosters and legitimates and thrives on violence from below and violence from above.

3. The taproot of violence is surely *silence,* of being vetoed and nullified and canceled so that we have no say in the future of the community or of our own lives. How odd, in the midst of a technological revolution offering broad communication, that serious input into our common future is increasingly limited and monopolized so that we cynically conclude that our say does not matter anyway. The silenced are increasingly like a driven, helpless, desperate two-year-old who, having no say, will enact a tantrum; and so the tantrums build in Northern Ireland and among the Palestinians and in our own abandoned cities. Or to take it more intimately, every time a neighbor gets a machine gun and kills seventeen neighbors, the next day the comment is sure to be, "I don't know; he lived alone, kept to himself, and never talked to anybody." And we collude in the silence, the abused protecting the abuser until the killing comes.

We of all people have the textual resources authorizing and legitimating and modeling *speech that breaks the silence* of violence and the violence of silence. At the very outset of our story, it says of our victimized mothers and fathers in Egypt, they groaned and cried out, and God heard and God saw and God knew and God remembered and God came down to save (Exod. 2:23-25). But unlike our high Calvinist notions of sovereignty, the break comes *from below* in the daring speech of the silenced. Out of that comes this richness of complaint psalms and lament psalms and psalms of rage and hate and resentment, the voice from below refusing the silence, speaking truth amidst power, speaking truth to holiness and evoking newness.[9] It is all there in the preacher's script. Except that the colluding church and we colluding preachers and our colluding hymnal committees cover the Psalms, enhance the silence, and foster in our naive ways more violence.

The antidotes to violence in the text of the preacher—the text of the church—are small and incidental and local, as the work of the preacher always is:

1. The *offer of bread* amid the material deprivation is told in little ways:

> When David [fled for his life] . . . Barzillai the Gileadite from Roge-lim brought beds, basins, and earthen vessels, wheat, barley, meal, parched grain, beans, lentils, honey and curds, sheep, and cheese from the herd, for David and the people with him to eat for they said, "The troops are hungry and weary and thirsty in the wilderness." (2 Sam. 17:27-29)

The gesture of Barzillai may have been calculated politics and military strategy. In the midst of that, though, the preacher can show that the narrative of public life depends on the concrete offer of bread that resists deprivation. What strikes me about the text is the quintessential human act of being sure that bread is passed to those who need bread, an act that anticipates by centuries the mandate:

> Is not this the feast that I choose . . .

> Is it not to share your bread with the hungry,
>   and to bring the homeless poor into your house? (Isa. 58:6-7)

The violence dissipates where natural linkages are made.

2. The affirmation of *covenantal solidarity* amidst social dissociation is rooted in the practice of God's own life:

> For the LORD your God is God of gods and Lord of lords, the great God, mighty, awesome, who is not partial and takes no bribe, who executes justice for the orphan and the widow, and who loves the strangers, providing them food and clothing. You shall also love the strangers for you were strangers in the land of Egypt. (Deut. 10:17-19)

Imagine Yahweh, the strongest one in the community, running a food pantry and collecting clothing for widows and orphans, physical gestures of solidarity that concretely and intensely bind the God of all creation to the undocumented workers and welfare recipients. In the end, Moses says, "You do it too."

3. The *legitimation of speech* in a context of enforced silence is given us even in the story of Jesus:

> Bartimaeus . . ., a blind beggar, was sitting by the roadside. When he heard that it was Jesus of Nazareth, he began to shout and say, "Jesus, Son of David, have mercy on me!" Many sternly ordered him to be quiet, but he cried out even more loudly, "Son of David, have mercy on me!" Jesus stood still and said, "Call him here." (Mark 10:46-49)

Jesus did not initiate the action. Bartimaeus pushed his way in. He pushed his way in by loud insistence while "many" shushed him. Perhaps "many" includes some disciples who were interested in a nice meeting. Health came to this blind man by abrasive insistence and disruption. Had he been finally shushed, moreover, at best there would have been no healing, at worst perhaps he would have begun throwing angry stones at Jesus and his bunch because he would have been refused access.

My point is not to focus on violence per se. I do so only because violence saturates the dominant textual versions of our social reality. That dominant version

- thinks *bread must be guarded,* and not shared
- thinks it is *each against all,* with no ground for community
- thinks *silence can authenticate the status quo*

Our best strategies for the maintenance of advantage carry with them the very seeds of upheaval and disruption. The preacher has the script and the burden and the chance of a sub-version of social reality, whereby bread and covenantal speech offer a humanity against violence. It strikes me afresh that the preacher's sub-version of reality is not given in large ideological slogans, but in small, dense, particular texts: a gesture by Barzillai with detail down to beans and lentils; a clothing drive for widows and orphans operated by the Lord of the Exodus; Bartimaeus the beggar who crowds into the doctor's office to demand and receive healing. These local, cherished memories seed our reimagining of reality outside the killing fields that the dominant version takes as normative.

IV

My theme is *alternative,* sub-version to version, the sermon a moment of alternative imagination, the preacher exposed as point man, point woman, to make up out of nothing more than our memory and our hope and our faith a radical option to the normalcy of deathliness. It occurs to me that the *scandal of particularity* so prominent in the election of Israel and so decisive in the incarnation of Jesus is pervasive in biblical faith, always so particular, always so peculiar, always so at odds. It occurs to me that the *Jewish imagination* of the Old Testament is so peculiar and so particular because Jews are always the odd men and women out, always at odds, always at risk, always in the presence of an empire with its insistent version of reality, always telling the boys and girls that we are different, different because we have been in the demanding presence of the Holy One, and now we must keep redeciding for a life propelled by that presence. The Jews, over time, devised signals of oddity—sabbath, kosher, circumcision.[10]

In parallel fashion, for like reasons, the baptismal imagination of the New Testament is so peculiar and so particular because Christians are

always odd men and women come together in odd communities and congregations, always at odds, always at risk, always in the presence of large
cultural empires that want to dissolve our oddity for reasons of state,
always telling the girls and boys we are different because we have been with
Jesus. We are forever reimagining and retelling and reliving our lives
through the scandal of Friday and the rumor of Sunday. We, like Jews,
devise signals of oddity, the notice of new life, the bread of brokenness, the
wine of blessedness, and the neighbor, always the neighbor, who is for us a
signal of the love of God.

The maintenance of oddity—which creates freedom for life, energy for
caring, and joy through the day—is the first task of the preacher. It spins off
into public policy and proposes reordered public life. But the first task is the
maintenance of oddity for the people in the room in the sound of the
preacher's voice. When an Old Testament teacher thinks about the maintenance of oddity, the inevitable beginning place is 2 Isaiah, not only for what
is said, but for what we imagine the context to be.

As some of you know, I have thought that in "the Christian West," the
baptized community is now in something like *exile*, a place I characterize as
hostile or indifferent to our primal faith claims.[11] So it is as in Babylon
when the Jewish prism of life was regarded as an imperial problem, or at
least an inconvenience. And so it is as in consumer-oriented capitalism in
the West, where the church is a cultural problem or at least an inconvenience. That is what the Babylonians thought, and the evidence is that
many of the Jews agreed. Many of the Jews found it too expensive or troublesome to maintain odd identity, because you could not get good jobs and
you could not get your kids into good schools. Consequently, giving up
oddity is a small price to pay for well-being offered by the empire.

Then there arises this daring chutzpah-filled poet who seeks to resist the
sellout of Jewishness and to foster and evoke and enhance the oddity. It is
his urging, in utterance after utterance, that odd Yahwistic identity is valid
and viable, because Yahweh, the key player in this odd identity, is back in
play in the empire. The power and persuasiveness of the dominant Babylonian version of reality had all but eliminated Yahweh, and nobody
thought Yahweh was a factor anymore. Yahweh becomes an available factor in the life of the community only through the daring utterance of the
poet. You know the sequence. The poet anticipates the overthrow of Babylon and its dominant version of reality through Cyrus the Persian. Cyrus is
an agent—so says the poet—of Yahweh, the real governor of world history.

The story line is given through a variety of rhetorical ventures, of which
I will comment on four. This poet is a daring preacher, and I want you to see
simply that given faith and given imagination, one can do almost anything
rhetorically.

1. *Isaiah 41:21-29*. The poet imagines, and creates before the imagination of the listening community of not quite convinced Jews, a law court.

That law court exists only on the lips of the poet, but the scene is vivid enough to last through eight verses, enough for twenty minutes if you talk slowly. Yahweh, the creator of heaven and earth, holds court. The question before the court is, *who is a true God?* The court summons the gods of Babylon for questioning. Those gods did not expect to be summoned by a Jewish court, but they are. They had been in charge so long they did not anticipate they would have to give a detailed account of themselves and so justify their claims.

In the court, the poet has Yahweh speak, in order to taunt the Babylonians. I suppose some Jews were fed up with Babylonian arrogance and would have liked to taunt but did not dare. And now the poet does it in the protected place of Jewish utterance. We can paraphrase this conversation. The gods of the empire are asked,

> Tell us what happened . . . silence;
> tell us what is to happen . . . silence;
> tell us what is to come hereafter . . . silence;
> do good . . . silence;
> do harm . . . silence;
> frighten us . . . silence.

These gods cannot say "boo."

> Verdict: you are nothing!
> your work is nothing!
> your worshipers are nothing!

Then Yahweh takes the stand; and Yahweh can talk! Yahweh has authority and energy and vitality. Unlike the silence of the empire, this irascible Yahweh can give evidence for Yahweh's claim:

> I stirred up Cyrus;
> I first declared it;
> I gave Jerusalem a herald of good tidings;
> No one helped;
> No one consoled;
> No one answered.

> Verdict: I am the real thing; they are empty wind.

The rhetoric is and is intended to be subversive. It addresses the imagination of Jews. It asserts that the military-industrial authority of Babylon cannot keep its promises, cannot make you happy, cannot make you safe. Yahweh is unlike all of this . . . particular, peculiar, scandalous, odd, resilient, reliable. Go Yahweh!

The result is modest as with most sermons. The Jews leave the place of utterance. There is a chance now that they will stay Jews, with freedom for action, with energy for caring, with resolve to stay odd. What is given in the liturgical moment of course is not known by Babylonian authorities. No doubt many in that meeting where they heard the daring poetry were ambivalent: why Jewish, why odd, why circumcised, why baptized? The evidence *out there* seems to be against the claims made *in here* for Yahweh, but the poet makes the claims anyway. The images offered haunt and haunt and will haunt, and will not quit.

2. *Isaiah 41:8-13.* In the same chapter of Isaiah, the God who speaks abrasively in the courtroom to expose the pitiful gods of the empire here speaks pastorally in the family. Here there are no Babylonians, only bewildered Jews, treasured people of Yahweh who thought they had been abandoned. The God of the exiles speaks:

> You, Israel, my servant,
>   Jacob, whom I have chosen,
> the offspring of Abraham, my friend
>   you whom I took from the ends of the earth,
> and called from its farthest corners,
>   saying to you, "You are my servant,
> I have chosen you and not cast you off."

The chosen in exile had almost forgotten and had almost been forgotten. It had been a long time since they had been called by their intimate names of faith, because in Babylon they were nothing more than imperial statistics.

And now speaks the God who remembers. This God names their names, their family names, the names of most intimate identity, and in doing so mobilizes the precious stories of promise in Genesis, situating these exiles among Jacob and Abraham who are friend, chosen, gathered. The poem is like the TV show *Cheers*—"where everybody knows your name!" Imagine, exiles have not been called by their baptismal names for a long time. For many exiles in this technological rat race, the church is the only place in town where everybody knows your name.

This God continues to speak, the most personal utterance we all crave, the one we first hear from our mothers. And now speaks the mothering God to the motherless exiles: "Fear not . . . Do not be afraid . . . I am with you . . . I am right here." Do not be afraid; I am your God. I am here in Babylon. I am here in exile. I am God here in the empire. You are not alone. Stay with me. This is an intimate word of assurance. It is an intimate word on the lips of the creator of heaven and earth, the one who authorizes oddity, the one who speaks the words the empire would most like to stop, because people mothered beyond fear are not so easily managed or administered or intimidated.

> I will strengthen you, I will help you;
> I will uphold you with my victorious right hand.
>   . . . those who war against you

shall be as nothing at all.
For I, the LORD your God,
    hold your right hand;
it is I who say to you, "Do not fear,
    I will help you."

This is only an utterance. It is only poetry. And then the Jews must leave their special place of poetry and imagination, some cynical, some bewildered, some touched, some sensing the strangeness . . . tingling, held, affirmed, empowered, not so downcast, not so bought off, not so compromised. And the Babylonians haven't a clue! They do not know about the strangeness that opens for newness through utterance. But it has been spoken. And here and there it has been heard.

3. *Isaiah 52:7-10.* The defeat of the Babylonians goes on in an imaged *courtroom.* The "fear not" of Yahweh is uttered in circles of *familial intimacy.* These two daring rhetorical strategies prepare the ground for *gospel,* the news uttered among exiles. It is this poet among our people who makes the word *gospel* into a core theological term. You know the text:

How beautiful upon the mountains
    are the feet of the messenger who announces *shalom,*
who brings good news,
    who announces salvation,
    who says to Zion . . . "Your God reigns."

The word is *gospel.* The good news as gospel is that Yahweh as God has just now regained governance.

The outcome is that Babylon has been defeated, Babylonian gods are weak, nothing to fear, nothing to lose, nothing to pay, nothing to joy. The news is that the Dominant Vision of reality has been defeated. The odd subversion of reality now has a chance. The sentinels lift up their voices, for they have been waiting and watching for a long time. The ruins of Jerusalem sing. The despairing dance. The desolate are in wonder. Because the odd God of this odd people in this odd version of reality has come to power.

It is gospel—but only a poetic moment among exiles. It is news—but not yet public. It is only liturgy, only utterance, only imagination. The same sort of liturgical utterance in imagination is offered when Jesus of Nazareth came to say, "the kingdom of God has come near; repent" (Mark 1:15). He just said it, and some believed and began a new trajectory of existence. Everything begins in the utterance.

4. *Isaiah 52:10-11.* So, says the poet, on the basis of the news, "depart, depart." Leave Babylon. Leave the dominant version of reality. Leave the place of fear and anxiety. Leave and head home to Jewishness, to obedience, to joy, to freedom. The gospel is an alternative to the dominant version of reality that is always reductive, endlessly robbing us of our humanness. The

way is clear for a seriously different way of life. The poem offers a future that can be taken up as we are able.

V

But of course this *gospel of departure* in the poetry of 2 Isaiah is only a retelling of the primal narrative of the exodus. The exodus narrative is not historical reportage. It is, rather, stylized liturgy in order that "you may tell your children in time to come." What you shall tell your children is:

- "We groaned . . . and cried out" (Exod. 2:23-25), going public in our protest against the dominant narrative version of reality that incessantly said, "Make more bricks."
- The technological program of Research and Development in ancient Egypt matched Yahweh's first two miracles (plagues). But we knew we had reached the outer limit of Egyptian technological capacity and the far reach of Egyptian power to make life possible when with the third event of this contest it was concluded, "[the Egyptians] could not" (Exod. 8:18).
- We danced the dance of new life at the edge of the waters, on the day Miriam and the other women took their tambourines and danced by the waters of liberation (Exod. 15:20-21).
- We watched while Yahweh "made sport" of Pharaoh, while Yahweh undid the power of Pharaoh (Exod. 10:1-2), and we noticed an opening for alternative existence outside the control of Pharaoh.

So we will tell our sons and daughters—and all those who will listen—that life under the demanding quotas and insistences of the empire is not the only way to have life. So we left; we walked through the waters of chaos, we reached dry land on the other side, we received the bread of miracle; we arrived finally at Sinai where we bound our life to the life of God and the life of the neighbor. We will tell our children about the darkness of Passover, so that they may know another life is possible in the world. The children will be astonished when they realize that the second book of our sacred canon is named "Departure." The dominant version of reality is undermined and subverted by the conviction that staying is not our own option. The liturgy is always authorizing an alternative humanity, and sometimes we go; sometimes we linger in wistful reluctance, wishing we had courage, sometimes choosing the fleshpots that enslave but knowing that in the end our belly is not our god (see Phil. 3:10).

VI

But of course, in Christian reading, the *gospel of departure* writ large in the exodus narrative and sung buoyantly in the lyrics of 2 Isaiah is but a long-term anticipation of the odd story of Jesus. As the story goes, Jesus came to those paralyzed by the demands of the overpunctilious requirements of some forms of Judaism that had been diverted from the claims of God and neighbor, and by the comprehensive ideology of the Roman government that wanted to eliminate the God of the Jews from its horizon. As the story goes, Jesus came among those frozen in narratives of anxiety and alienation, of slavery and fear; he authorized a departure into the new world of God's governance. He appeared abruptly, and he said, "Repent—turn—change—switch, for the new governance is at hand."

And then he acted it out, summoning, forgiving, instructing, cleansing, healing, empowering, feeding. The new governance given in the very person of Jesus brings all of life—public and personal, human and nonhuman—into a regime of wholeness. He came with a mandate to do for the world what the Creator had intended from the outset. He found it all there in the scroll that authorized him:

> "The Spirit of the Lord is upon me,
> because he has anointed me
> to bring good news to the poor.
> He has sent me to proclaim release to the captives
> and recovery of sight to the blind,
> to let the oppressed go free,
> to proclaim the year of the Lord's favor."
>   (Luke 4:18-19; cf. Isa. 61:1)

Those who were settled deep in the dominant version of reality tried to kill him. They recognized immediately that their big version of reality is here subverted.

He subverted by his mercy miracles what they had declared impossible. He sub-versioned by his emancipatory teaching—which was not quite clear (parabolic) but marked by quixotic irony—as though mocking the way it had been for a long time. He seemed to authorize and invite a rethinking of reality and eventually a reliving of reality. Those who had been with him were restored to their sanity and began to live in ways that the world could not bear. His sub-version sounded familiar cadences, but it was never quite the same. As a result, John—bold, unintimidated, direct John, bewildered and genuinely uncertain—sent word from prison: "Are you for real?"

Ever cagey as an evangelical subversive must always be, Jesus refused a direct answer. How could he answer such a big question in such a restrictive context, because the creeds had not been formulated that would provide him with a firm *homoousia* ("of one substance") identity? So he answers John from the data at hand: "Go and tell John what you have seen and heard: the blind receive their sight, the lame walk, lepers are cleansed, the deaf hear, the dead are raised, the poor have good news brought to them (Luke 7:22). Go tell John: new life swirls around me. Go tell John that where

I am present, impossible things happen. Go tell John that people are switching over to my narrative because they are worn out by blindness and want to see, they are tired of deadness and want to live. Go tell John a new world is being birthed among those who no longer accept dominant notions of the possible.

That sub-version of course constitutes a threat to the way things are. It is a threat that must be stopped by action of the state or whatever action that is available to us, violent if necessary. But go tell John, the stoppage of new life and the triumph of the dominant version lasted only thirty-six hours and no more. Because by Sunday new life was turned loose beyond the frightened, confined ways of the conventional. That new power has stayed loose, sometimes retarded, sometimes domesticated, but ever loose in the world, breaking bonds, shattering closures in order to,

> bring down the powerful from their thrones
>   and lift up the lowly,
> filling the empty with good things
>   and sending the rich empty away.
>   (Luke 1:52-53, my paraphrase)

This odd community has continued to reflect upon, to practice, and to invite others into this account of reality. Most of the data on which we count and to which we cling is local and specific. There have been among us, however, those eloquent lyricists capable of larger articulation. One among us has gone very large indeed to assert:

> He is the image of the invisible God, the firstborn of all creation; for in him all things in heaven and on earth were created, things visible and invisible, whether thrones or dominions or rulers or powers— all things have been created through him and for him. He himself is before all things, and in him all things hold together. (Col. 1:15-17)

The claim is stupendous. But what we have found, generation after generation, is that we could not cease to make claims, even as we could not cease to ponder and engage in new practices, always dangerous, always at the cusp of new life.

VII

I say things you already have long known. We keep meeting to say them to one another because, if left unsaid, the old powers of death creep back in and take over. We say them to one another because we depend on the fresh utterance to give fresh edge of possibility to our lives. We say these things to one another because the utterances mediate the Easter option . . . without these utterances there is no such option.

The sense of this utterance, in which we preachers are participants,is that an alternative world is possible. The old world is not a given; it is a fraud. Another world is possible—*in our imaginations:* we listen and imagine differently. In our liberation we entertain different realities not yet given in hardware, so far only very soft ware, carried only by narrative and song and poem and oracle, said before being embodied, but said and we listen. As we listen we push out to the possibility and are held by it like a visioning child with a dream.

Another world is possible—*in our practice.* We are only a few, but we are some. We can do little, but something. As we stay with the cadences of our defining utterance, we begin to enact another world. Foolishly we enact obedience to a daring claim, obedience to a possibility; we specialize in cold water and shared bread, in welcome speech, hospitality, sharing, giving, compassion, caring, in small ways, setting the world fresh.

Another world is possible—we imagine—in public policy, for we do not doubt that the small deed—here and there—ripples into reallocated funds, redirected vision, reassigned power that issues in caring health, in mercy as policy, in peace that overrides war, in hope that overcomes poverty. This is not often possible, however, because of the stubbornness of Caesar and the intransigence of corporate wealth. But we have enough public access because we are no longer contained in old tired refusals.

> We listen and we answer.
> If we are Black enough, we may say "Amen" and "my, my";
> if we are Episcopal, we may say "ummmm";
> if we are frozen Calvinists, we may not answer,
> but only ponder and then act.

In all our several ways of answering, we calculate the possibilities and move to the sub-version—sometimes as tough as nails. We refuse dominant versions of reality, seeing the flow of newness and acknowledging the chance.

We are indeed a *sub-people* . . . sub-versive, sub-verted, sub-verting, sub rosa, subtle. We are on the ground, underneath official versions. Our subness is rooted, in our pain, because you cannot fool pain; in our hope, because hope comes without our permission.

But after our pain and after our hope, the rootage of our *sub* is in God's holiness, a holiness we have seen and trusted, whose name we know, a holiness untamed, thick, abrasive—newness unashamed.

A final text, *Acts 3:11-16.* Peter and John had just authorized a lame man to walk. They said to him, we are told, "In the name of Jesus Christ of Nazareth, stand up and walk . . . " (v. 6) We are told, "Jumping up, he stood and began to walk, and he entered the temple with them, walking and leaping and praising God." It was not supposed to happen. But it did.

The people were astonished. But Peter answered simply: "Why do you stare at us, as though our power or our piety we had made him walk? . . .

It is not us, but faith in his name. To this we are witnesses" (vv. 12-16, my paraphrase). And witnesses and witnesses and witnesses. Not more than that, but surely not less than that.

℗ 2

Life-or-Death,
De-Privileged Communication

IT STRIKES ME THAT THE MOST IMPORTANT FACT ABOUT PREACHING IN THE contemporary U.S. church is that proclamation of the gospel is no longer a privileged claim. That is, it can no longer assume or appeal to a broadly based consensus that dominates our culture. By that, I do not refer to the fact of pluralism that is unarguable, nor to the loss of institutional clout for the church, nor to the erosion of the social authority of the pastor, though all of these realities surely are important.

Rather, I refer to the recognition we must face that construal of the world *without reference to God* is intellectually credible and socially acceptable as it never has been before in European-American culture. I suppose one can say that such assumed atheism (no god) or embraced idolatry (distorted god) is the final victory of Enlightenment consciousness.[1] But that victory has come about, so it seems to me, rather unintentionally and issues in vulgar, unexamined forms.

The upshot of that changed intellectual, social climate is that preaching has to start "farther back," because nothing is conceded by the listening assembly at the outset. This is obviously true for people who have long since given up on gospel claims of the church, either because these claims are misunderstood through stereotypes of superstition or coercion or because these claims are rightly understood as too costly and too disruptive of a self-focused life. But more important, it appears to me that in some large measure, "nothing is conceded" even in the baptismal community, for even baptized people (including perhaps you, dear reader, and me as writer) have learned to construe the real practice of our lives without reference to the claims of God. Thus the beginning is not in *assent*, but at the most, in open *wonderment* and perhaps, down deep, in hidden, resentful *resistance*.

In such a social environment, it is evident that a different mode of preaching and different expectations on the part of the preacher may be important. The de-privileging of the claims of the sermon repositions the sermon (and the preacher) in terms of communication. My suggestion, growing out of my recent study of Old Testament theology, is that the genre of *testimony* (as bid for assent), rather than *proclamation* (on an assumption of universal consensus), is how ancient Israel proceeded to claim truth in a like situation.[2] It is how we might, I suggest, rethink the genre of the sermon.

I understand that the term *testimony* in staid Calvinist ears, for example, calls to mind emotive, primitive religious talk among certain Baptists that is not well informed or well disciplined. In ancient usage, however, *testimony* refers not to religious emoting. It refers rather to a courtroom exercise in which the "truth of the matter" is deeply contested and different witnesses are called upon to give accounts of "the truth of the matter" that turn out to be profoundly contradictory. The recent trials of O. J. Simpson and Timothy McVeigh make available to us a social environment of *contested truth with competing bids for assent.*

With the loss of Christian consensus and theological hegemony, "the truth of the matter" is greatly contested, the truth about the reality and character of God and the consequent reality and character of the world. There was a time of consensus in the West when the preacher could speak from high philosophical and moral ground simply to reiterate "what we all believe." Now, however, the preacher offers a construal of reality that sits alongside other construals of God and world reality, each of which has its adherents and its points of credibility.[3]

The *dethroning of Christian privilege* and the need for the risk of testimony are perhaps illuminated by citing three examples of testimony as *bids for assent:*

1. Elie Wiesel has spent his life in determination that the barbaric reality of the Jewish holocaust shall not be forgotten. He has observed that the truth of the Holocaust is deeply disputed and there are those who insist it never happened. More than that, he has observed that the truth of the Holocaust depends completely upon the witnesses, people who are not sophisticated but who are credible through the character of their testimony, through their capacity to tell credibly how it was with them.[4]

2. A great deal of attention has been given to the practice of "stories of woundedness" among those who are ill and who require medical attention. "Scientific medicine," rather like "consensus theological truth," has had no need of stories, because it operated out of the "truth of medicine" that was established "from above," as was theological truth. Without denying the important claims of scientific medicine, more recent observers have noticed that suffering people need to tell the story of suffering so as to engage others in a relatedness of suffering whereby healing may happen as a relational phenomenon. Indeed, in his book *The Wounded Storyteller,* Arthur Frank has offered a chapter entitled "testimony," giving evidence of the ways a sufferer must construe reality "from below," that is, out of pain.[5]

3. The other day I was in a bank teller line at noon, observing to the woman next to me in line how most bank tellers took long lunch breaks just when I wanted one to be available. That comment triggered in the woman behind me, whom I did not know, the opportunity for her to tell me her story of being cheated by a fast-food place out of fifty dollars of low-pay wages and to report that she never got a lunch break. She then told me that she planned to bring a suit against the company for having cheated her. She said, "I will probably lose, but I will have been heard." She told me that message three times in four minutes. She was giving "testimony," and she

would give more of it in court, stating her bid for truth. It was, moreover, urgent that she be heard, even if the fast-food company would be dominant in court, as she herself anticipated. She will have been heard with her version of truth!

Notice in all three cases, testimony comes as a truth "from below" in the face of a "stronger truth" that is hegemonic:

- Jewish *survivors* amid scientific analysis of what happened
- *sufferers* amid medical science
- the *"cheated woman"* in the face of a powerful fast-food chain

Each of these witnesses makes a bid for a version of the truth.

Such testimony is characteristically:[6]

- *Fragile.* It depends upon the nerve of the teller.
- *Local.* It makes no sweeping, universal claim but appeals to what is concretely known.
- *Persuasive.* The rhetorical casting aims at winning the jury.
- *Contested.* It dares utterance in the presence of other claims that may be more powerful and more credible.
- *Fragmented.* It is only a bit of a narrative that brings with it a whole theory of reality that is implied but left unexpressed.

Such claims for truth are not loud, arrogant, or sweeping. They are modest but insistent and sometimes compelling. The connection of *testimony-trial-truth-jury* means that truth is not available ahead of time, before the utterance. It is available only after, through the utterance, when the jury reaches its verdict. So it is with the sermon, when the sermon is de-positioned from the judge's bench to the witness box.

II

It has occurred to me that the Old Testament is essentially de-privileged testimony that construes the world alternatively.[7] It is de-privileged because it is the evidence offered by a community that is early *nomads* or *peasants* and that is late a community of *exiles*. Either way, as peasants or as exiles, Israel lives a great distance from the great hegemonic seats of power and the great centers of intellectual-theological certitude. Israel always comes into the great courtroom of public opinion and disrupts the court in order to tell a tale of reality that does not mesh with the emerging consensus that more powerful people have put together.

At the center of this odd account of reality is this character Yahweh, whom Pharaoh does not know (Exod. 5:2) and whom the winners in the world by and large ignore. It is this strange God—so this testimony asserts—who comes among barren women to give births (Gen. 21:1-7), who comes into slave camps to set free (Exod. 15:20-21), who sends bread from heaven into wilderness contexts of hunger (Exod. 16:13-18), who governs the rise and fall of great powers (1 Sam. 2:6-8), who places widows, orphans, and illegal aliens at the center of the economic-political debate (Deut. 24:17-22; Isa. 1:17).

Israel on occasion will tell of this holy fidelity that is textured with impatient violence *to outsiders,* inviting others to join in doxology to this odd character:

> Praise the LORD, all you nations,
>> Extol him, all you peoples! (Ps. 117:1; cf. Ps. 67:3-5)

It is an odd *chutzpah*-filled invitation to ask nations and peoples to join to sing of this alternative reality on the basis of *local* experience:

> For great is his steadfast love toward us,
>> and the faithfulness of the LORD endures forever. (v. 2)

More characteristically Israel tells this peculiar version of reality to *its own children,* intending that this offbeat testimony at the center of this community will persist as a viable social force into the next generation:

> When in the future your child asks you, "What does this mean?" you shall answer, "By strength of hand the LORD brought us out of Egypt, from the house of slavery. When pharaoh stubbornly refused to let us go, the LORD killed all the firstborn in the land of Egypt, from human firstborn to the firstborn of animals. Therefore I sacrifice to the Lord every male that first opens the womb, but every firstborn of my sons I redeem." It shall serve as a sign on your hand and as an emblem on your forehead that by strength of hand the LORD brought us out of Egypt. (Exod. 13:14-16)

Most regularly, however, this *testimony of alternative truth* is offered to members of the community by members of the community. The purpose of such incessant testimony is to nurture and sustain one another in odd vision, because without such nurture and sustenance, it is for sure that members of the community will fall out of this truth into other more attractive, more palatable, less costly truth.

III

The clearest evidence for this process of testimony, I take it, is the poetry of 2 Isaiah (Isaiah 40–55). This poetry, it is commonly agreed, is uttered to Jewish exiles who have been deported to Babylon and who must practice their faith and their countertruth in a world of Babylonian hegemony. It is unmistakable that Babylon was not only a political-military superpower. It was also an advanced, sophisticated, winsome culture with its own theological rationale and its own moral justifications. Over time, the powerful attractiveness of Babylon must have been deeply compelling to many Jews.

Into this context of *seduction and resistance* comes the preacher-poet, 2 Isaiah. I cite only one pair of verses that evidence the contested, demanding situation of Jewish faith in the empire:

> Do not fear, or be afraid;
>> have I not told you from of old and declared it?
>> *You are my witnesses!*
> Is there any god besides me?
>> There is no other rock; I know not one.
>>>> (Isa. 44:8, emphasis mine)

In this brief assurance and summons offered by Yahweh, there are three identifiable components:

1. Israel—Jews in exile—are summoned and identified as *witnesses for Yahweh*. Witnesses do not come to court neutrally. They are "friendly" or "hostile," summoned either by the prosecution or the defense. Israel is summoned and authorized to come to the court of public opinion in order to line out to the court the Yahweh version of reality and to bid for assent to this truth.

2. The *witness is instructed*. A good attorney briefs the witness; so Yahweh instructs Israel as witness to assert in court that "Yahweh is the only one," that Yahweh is a rock without any competitors.[8]

3. Most astonishingly, Yahweh *assures the witness* Israel, "Do not fear; do not be afraid." The situation is not unlike a fragile person who goes to an attorney in the secret of the night with evidence that will blow the case open. But that evidence is dangerous, and the witness will be at risk. In order not to lose the testimony (and consequently the case) because of fearfulness, the attorney assures the witness that "it will be all right." In Babylon, it was hazardous to the health of Israel to witness to Yahweh and so to contradict the massive Babylonian claim to legitimacy and absoluteness. No wonder the witness must be reassured, "Do not fear."

Jews exist, so says this poetry, to make the case in the empire for a different truth, a different presentation of reality, a different basis for humanness in the world. The case to be made in court by Israel is, of course, not uncontested. So the text goes on to say,

> All who make idols are nothing, and the things they delight in do not profit; their witnesses neither see nor know. And so they will be put to shame. (v. 9)

The empire also has its gods. And those gods also have witnesses. And those witnesses come into court as well, to make their polished, sophisticated case before the court. One would expect, of course, that these witnesses would offer compelling testimony for the empire, because they have all of the best evidence, the slickest lawyers, the best research, the most compelling style. Except, says the text, they are *tôhû;* they are embodiments of chaos, agents of disorder who are blind and deaf. They are hopeless witnesses advocating a hopeless truth.

And so the issue is joined in court. The poetry does not pay much attention to the evidence brought by Babylonian witnesses, instead treating it all as a weak joke (44:9-20). Rather, all the energy goes to the testimony to be given by Israel, for a countertruth about a counter-God with a counterethic in the world.

1. This testimony by Israel offers a past that is saturated with *life-giving miracles,* not a past filled with self-sufficient achievement. So the poet appeals to Abraham and Sarah, a test case in Israel's memory, for the ways in which this God could take this hopeless old couple and create a vibrant community:

> Look to the rock from which you were hewn,
>   and to the quarry from which you were dug.
> Look to Abraham your father
>   and to Sarah who bore you;
> for he was but one when I called him,
>   but I blessed him and made him many.
>   (Isa. 51:1-2; see Heb. 11:11-12)

From that testimony derives a claim that we live in a world of life-giving miracles, not to be matched or stopped by the empire.

2. This testimony from Israel offers a future that is marked by *circumstance-defying promises* completely freed from the present tense that is too sober. So it is promised:

> For the mountains may depart and the hills be removed,
> but my steadfast love shall not depart from you,
>   and my covenant of peace shall not be removed,
>   says the Lord, who has compassion on you.
>
> O afflicted one, storm-tossed, and not comforted,
>   I am about to set your stones in antimony,
>   and lay your foundations with sapphires.
> I will make your pinnacles of rubies,
>   your gates of jewels,
>   and all your wall of precious stones.
> All your children shall be taught by the Lord,
>   and great shall be the prosperity of your children.
> In righteousness you shall be established;
>   you shall be far from oppression, for you shall not fear;
>   and from terror, for it shall not come near you.
>   (Isa. 54:10-14)

> For you shall go out in joy,
>> and be led back in peace . . .
> Instead of the thorn shall come up the cypress;
>> instead of the brier shall come up the myrtle.
>> (Isa. 55:12-13)

From this testimony emerges a future of complete *shalom* that is free of violence, brutality, competitiveness, and scarcity, a new governance that displaces that of the empire.

3. This testimony offers *a present tense filled with neighbors* to whom we are bound in fidelity, in obligation, and in mutual caring. Everywhere on the lips of this witness is the term *justice*, which entails inclusiveness for all those that the empire finds objectionable and unproductive:

> I have put my Spirit upon him;
>> he will bring forth *justice* to the nations.
> He will not cry or lift up his voice,
>> or make it heard in the street;
> a bruised reed he will not break,
>> and a dimly burning wick he will not quench;
>> he will faithfully bring forth *justice*.
> He will not grow faint or be crushed
>> until he has established *justice* in the earth;
> and the coastlands wait for his [Torah].
>> (Isa. 42:1-4, emphasis mine)

Thus appeal is made:
- *a past* of life-giving miracles
- *a future* of circumstance-denying promise
- *a present* tense of neighbors in fidelity

This testimony matters. It matters to stay in this truth. It matters to practice this version of life. And of course the imperial thought police, present in every preaching situation, recognize that it matters. It matters because the members of this odd community will not give in to the blandishments of the empire and so will remain an emancipated, unintimidated counterculture in the empire. It matters beyond that because even the agents of the empire occasionally recognize the credible character of this talk that will eventually subvert and collapse the empire.[9]

The preaching office is an office of an alternative truth that makes its bid for assent. It does so, moreover, in the face of the empire that wants to stop talk of *miracles, promises, and neighbors,* because such talk runs against the grain of imperial, ruthless self-sufficiency. And thus sooner or later—as every preacher knows—agents of the status quo will move in to halt the countertruth. They may be friendly or hard, open or covert. But they will try. Against such a risk, the sender says, "Fear not."

IV

It is my hunch that, give or take a little, every preaching context, every preaching occasion, is something like that. The preaching of the gospel is not the voice of the dominant empire but instead offers a truthfulness that may be confrontational or subtle, but instead eventually conflicts with imperial truth. I have no doubt that it is emancipatory for the preacher to recognize our actual preaching context that, in the past Christian West, is unprecedented. We are de-privileged but thereby free, because we need no longer carry water for the empire as was a given in a previous power arrangement.

This sense of being de-privileged recently struck me powerfully. I read in the *New York Times* a report on the violent military-social revolution in Sierra Leone.[10] The *Times* carried a picture of a soldier holding back a protesting crowd. The crowd of young people in that disadvantaged situation faced the power of status quo soldiers. They were waiting eagerly and impatiently for food. And on one of the young lads was a Nike cap.

And then I thought, Nike, with its U.S. heroes of Tiger Woods and Michael Jordan and its complementary Asian sweatshops, has become a universal symbol for greed and individual exploitation. (I do not single out Nike or Tiger or Michael, except as they embody in the most effective way the dominant truth of privatized success offered to the young.) It is astounding, in my judgment, that the Nike "swoosh" has become a universal symbol for success and well-being even without any verbalization. It is a symbol worn by unthinking, affluent suburbanites. It is a symbol worn by poor people in third-world economies who can for a moment entertain a fantasy. It is a symbol worn by the baptized so narcotized that we do not notice the irony.

In the world of Nike, moreover, the cross is a lonesome symbol of costly self-giving for the neighbor. (The cross on the wane perhaps has a companion in the waning of the hammer and sickle of Marxian thought that cannot withstand Nike and the crescent of Islam that cannot withstand Nike.)

And so the preacher must stand up and tell the truth in an environment where Nike seems a given and where many "Jewish exiles" submit to Babylonian truth without any awareness what such submission costs for our baptism. When the contradiction between the symbols and between sworn accounts of reality are exposed, imperial agents will be quick to move. In the world of "swoosh," preaching the Crucified One is a dangerous business, profoundly de-privileged.

It is de-privileged communication, of that there can be no doubt. But such preaching is, I have no doubt, life or death. Because what this gospel asserts matters to our common future:

- It matters if *life-giving miracles* are scuttled for the sake of can-do achievements.

- It matters if *circumstance-denying promises* are silenced for the sake of winning at all costs.
- It matters if *bonded neighbors* are excommunicated in a passion for private *shalom*.

It matters because the makers of phony cultural icons are *tôhû*, agents of chaos, manufacturers of disorder that brings nothing but abusive trouble among brothers and sisters (Isa. 44:9). It matters! The preacher and the sermon are life or death and deeply de-privileged. In the face of that danger with such a freighted alternative truth, the poet says, "Do not fear."

⟨๏ 3

Together in the Spirit —
Beyond Seductive Quarrels

EVERYONE NOW AGREES THAT WE ARE AT A NEW SEASON IN THE LIFE OF THE U.S. church, a new season that is starkly different from what was but that has almost taken us by surprise. That new season of dislocation is surely to be seen as a profound challenge to the church. It is, moreover, widely felt, not without reason, to be a serious threat. It may also turn out to be a marvelous invitation for newness together that moves past old postures that predictably, perhaps inevitably, produced quarrels. The massive and unarguable dislocation of the conventional institutional church may be an occasion for a common resubmission to the power of God's Spirit.

One important aspect of that new season in the church is to rethink mission in a post-Christian society. I suspect that such a rethinking may permit church folk to move past the deep tension that arises when we think of mission in conventional ways, the tension between "evangelism" and "social action."

That tension is an old one, one that grows out of a deep misunderstanding. It will not, I imagine, surprise you that my thesis is this:

> To posit tension between evangelism and social action amounts to a deep distortion of both and is in the end a phony issue. Or to put it positively, serious, responsible faith attends to both serious evangelism and intentional social action.

If we are to work past this distorting antithesis, we shall have to go behind both; and what we find behind both mandates is the God of the Bible, the God of Israel decisively present in the story of Jesus. It is this God who is the principle subject of evangelism and the principle agent of social action. But before we leap to our certitude about these matters, we must recognize how difficult this God is as subject and as agent, difficult enough that we may not be too certain about our preferred extrapolations.

My way of formulating the God of the Bible is this:

> In the Bible God is shown to be endlessly irascible, given to us in deeply elusive texts that evidently require a polyphonic reading.

Now if we pay attention to the three deliberate adjectives in this characterization—irascible, elusive, polyphonic—it is immediately and abundantly clear that we may not be all too sure as we rush to the normative formulations of Christian faith and surely not all too certain as we embrace our favorite elements of church policy and practice.

It belongs to responsible, critical theological reflection to wait and to listen and to be surprised and subverted, and only then to move into our question of dispute. It is this God—marked by irascibility, elusiveness, and polyphonic dimension—who is the subject of evangelism and the agent of social action.

1

It is this *God who is the subject of the evangel,* the news that deabsolutizes every other claim of authority and that invites us to situate our lives in an odd narrative construal of the world, and therefore to live our lives according to a certain freedom and a certain danger. The evangel in the Old Testament is variously articulated:

- as the gift of freedom to depart the labor quotas of Pharaoh (Exodus);
- as the offer of covenant in rejection of the gods beyond the River (Joshua);
- as the invitation of homecoming in order to depart the demands of Babylon (2 Isaiah); and
- as the newness of joy, health, and thanks as an alternative to isolation, rejection, and fearfulness (Psalms).

The text, in its elusive, polyvocal cadences, endlessly asserts that the world is not closed according to the socio-political-economic or emotional hegemonies of the day. Rather, because of Yahweh's powerful intentionality, room and energy are provided for an alternative life in the world. This is the conviction and assurance about which Israel sings and dances in every circumstance of its life and in every generation of its existence.

This announcement of a chance for an alternative life in the world is the substance of the Christian gospel as it is of the gospel already given in the primary theological affirmations of the Old Testament to ancient Israel and through Israel to the surrounding peoples. It is always news that comes to us as a surprise. It is always good news because this alternative life in the world is characteristically better, more adequate, and more joyous than the old life conducted under the regimes of death.

The evangel is an offer of a *new baptismal identity* that makes us odd and free and able. It is my judgment that because evangelism bespeaks this alternative-generating God, it is important to accent in *baptismal identity* that the break between what was and what is now given is sharp and radical and wondrous and dangerous:

- It is an embrace of a deep memory to displace conventional amnesia, a memory filled with wondrous instances of miraculous transformations.
- It is an embrace of an exuberant hope to displace conventional despair

that besets both the endlessly afflicted and the comfortably complacent.

- It is an embrace of neighborliness that displaces conventional self-preoccupations that are grounded in anxiety and that eventuate in careless brutality and aggressive exploitation.

Of course that at its best is what baptismal identity has always been about, which is why immersion into the waters of death has always been a sign of the embrace of the gospel, a genuine relinquishment of old ways and a reception of a new way in the world that is wondrous and demanding.

In our own time and place, that baptismal offer, so it seems to me, is the offer of a construal of our lives and of all reality that is sharply alternative to the promises and demands of *military consumer capitalism,* which seeks to control us all, liberal and conservative; in our time and place, moreover, we may rightly wonder if life outside the contours of military consumer capitalism is possible, or even imaginable. But then such a wonderment has always been a core preoccupation of our mothers and fathers in the baptismal community:

- Is life imaginable beyond Pharaoh and his bread supply, even if it is the bread of affliction?
- Is life imaginable beyond the administration of Babylon, a provision of order even if an abusive order?
- Is life possible beyond our alienation and hates and fears and beyond the resulting destructive greed toward neighbor?

At its best, baptismal identity is like that. We, however, are in the sorry, silly situation we are in about evangelism because the substance and claims of the evangel have been so trivialized that we tend to miss the point. As a consequence, it comes about, surely since the settlement of Constantine, that baptismal evangelism has not been so wondrous or so dangerous, but has been reduced to joining an institution that is powerfully allied with the status quo. In our latter days of secularism, moreover, it has been further reduced to "church growth" and the recruitment of numbers in order to sustain and prosper the body. There is, I am sure, nothing intrinsically wrong with church growth as an intentional enterprise, one already practiced by the apostles in the book of Acts. Unless it is practiced in ways that simply reinforce our already accommodated life: our most intimate interpersonal, familial, sexual matters and our most public practices of economics and social policy whereby we are distinguished from "those less fortunate"—rather than the insistence that the God of the gospel makes all things new. When the God of the Bible is the subject of the evangel, it means that every aspect and dimension of our lives is being brought under the rule and intention of that God. The news is that the required *relinquishment* and *receiving* is both possible and positive.

II

The God who is the subject of the evangel is the God who is *the decisive agent of social action.* It is God's crucial nature in what we have come to call social action that may deliver the social action of some liberals from an ideological quality. It is the sustained affirmation of the Bible that the creator of heaven and earth is at work to mend and redeem and repair and rehabilitate the world so that it may become the good creation . . . the new creation . . . that God has always and everywhere intended. It is the great temptation of so-called social activists to imagine that "God has no hands but ours," and if we do not do it, then it will not be done. Such a notion is completely antithetical to the ways in which the God of the Bible is shown to be at work in the world.

An important check on that mistaken notion, a check that makes all our zeal penultimate, is the awareness and acknowledgment that God is indeed effectively at work on behalf of the well-being of the world. This is the God,

> who executes justice for the oppressed;
>   who gives food to the hungry.
> The LORD sets the prisoners free;
>   the LORD opens the eyes of the blind.
> The LORD lifts up those who are bowed down;
>   The LORD loves the righteous.
> The LORD watches over the strangers;
>   he upholds the orphan and the widow,
>   but the way of the wicked he brings to ruin.
> The LORD will reign forever.
>   (Ps. 146:7-10)

God is, even as we speak, doing the work of bringing the entire world under his good rule. God, moreover, will not quit until it is finished. So the Psalm concludes with an expectant, confident doxology:

> The Lord will reign forever,
>   your God, O Zion, for all generations.
> Praise the LORD!

The conviction of those evangelized in this hymn that God is at work is what brings the world to *shalom.*

It is evident, even on the surface, that the world is not yet at God's *shalom?* We are not agreed on how to think about that undeniable reality. One way is to focus upon "original sin" and imagine that it is long-term human sin that has brought the world to its present sorry state, and that there can be no doubt of human implication in that condition. Another way to think about our condition—one toward which I am inclined—is to notice the *resilient power of chaos* (and the devil) in the world that is not yet subdued or governed by God.[1] Or a third way is to conclude that *God's own self is not finally reliable* but is sometimes abusive and so contributes in huge ways to the trouble so massive among us.[2]

However we may understand the large theological root of our manifest problems in the world, there is much yet to be done, and those who enter into the Yahweh narrative by way of baptism are inescapably engaged in the work of mending the world that is God's own work. We are engaged *by prayer,* whereby we pray daily that God's way of governance shall be fully established on earth as it already is in heaven so that there will be no more violence, poverty, homelessness, nor any other injustice. We are engaged *in hope,* whereby each day we expect God's decisive action, fully confident that things need not stay the way they are and will not stay the way they are, simply because God is God. As in prayer and hope, we are engaged in God's transformative work in the world by *our actions*—when we make our intentional, bodily investments in the narrative of God that we have, in baptismal identity, come to accept as the true story of our own lives. We invest our bodies in this way, not because it is exceptional or because it is heroic or because it especially moral or virtuous, but because it is the natural and unexceptional living out of who we are in our relished identity as members of the narrative of God.

Having subscribed to this narrative identity in the act of baptism, a narrative identity situated in the large narrative of God, we live out a life of justice in terms of concrete neighbor concern and in terms of social policy and large sociopolitical questions. The new identity that makes such a life possible and that commands such a life is rooted in the dramatic act of baptism and in the slow nurture of baptismal growth.

The best example known to me of the natural and unexceptional living out of who we are is in the evangelical community of Le Chambeau, a French village led by the Huguenot pastor Andre Trocmé.[3] It is the tale of a small community that quietly, unobtrusively, and at great risk hid many Jews during the height of the brutality of National Socialism in central Europe. Later on, one of the young Jewish children hidden there, now an adult, returned to the village to investigate and interview people in order to discover their motivations for the risks they had run. The responses he received to his queries were inarticulate shrugs of the shoulder. There were no special reasons. There were no great ideals or heroic notions. There was simply nonchalance about who the community is in the gospel. They answered, "We did it because it did not occur to us that we should not." That radical social action was only the public articulation of baptismal identity. Social action indwells the evangel because the God who *promises the news of the gospel* is the God at work *transforming the world,* inviting all adherents of the gospel to share in the transformational work.

Thus, when it is confessed that God is *the subject of the evangel* and God is *the agent of social action,* no division between the two is thinkable. The division or tension between the two is possible only when evangelism is trivialized away from God and when social action is undertaken in Promethean autonomy. Evangelism taken by itself becomes *self-indulgent narcissism* that imagines our embrace of the gospel to be an end in itself rather than enlistment in an alternative world. Social action by itself becomes *hard-nosed ideology* that is authoritarian and graceless. My sense is that social-action types must always be regospeled, that is, reevangelized, reinvited into the news so that the action stays God's and not ours. And thus our action may stay buoyant, propelled not by success but by faithfulness. Simple summary: people on all sides of the question must keep our imagination singularly focused on the irascible God given us in elusive, polyphonic modes, lest we cast lots to divide up God's seamless garment of passionate sovereignty, divide up according to our several vested interests.

III

Having made a theological urging about the twin accents of evangelism and social action as they are both facets of God's own work and consequently nonnegotiable facets of our life in faith, I want to reflect a bit historically upon this odd split in the modern world. I am no historian and so will not vouch for my reading, which is only impressionistic.

It seems to me self-evident that all through the life of the Constantinian church, neither evangelism nor social action was a high priory in the West and did not need to be. Evangelism was not necessary, because all were born into Christian culture and state churches. In parallel fashion social action was not necessary because princes were Christian and, at least in modest ways (but in ways sharply contrasted with modern market-driven governments), practiced a social concern, albeit in deeply hierarchical ways.

It seems plausible to suggest that with the rise of modernity—the Thirty Years War that divided Europe, the rise of science that produced church responses filled with anxiety and aggressive certitude, and the emergence of an Enlightenment epistemology—our twin issues began to surface and take on importance and generate passion. It became intellectually evident and culturally obvious that church membership and Christian social ethics are not primordial givens, but at a minimum are choices that may nor may not be chosen. As a consequence, the embrace of Christian faith and membership in the church very gradually became a matter of individual choice, and as public ethics became increasingly secular and alienated from the claims of the gospel, the fabric of a Christian social ethic was no longer a given but only a goal able to be chosen and a possible strategy for social order.

That is, it is the waning of long-term Christian hegemony in Christendom that has produced this current agenda and this profound tension within the life of the church. The practical effect, so it seems to me, has been to drive "credible" Christianity away from public issues and to focus upon a privatized familial agenda as the proper work of the gospel and as the credible zone of God's governance. Such a development thus produced a kind of individualized, privatized "evangelical self" that is acutely modern, and a reactive response of public ethics (social action) that is equally modern in its shape. That is, the tension so evident to us, I suggest, is a remarkable result of Enlightenment consciousness that has made the gospel *awkwardly* "other" in our belated context, that invites a private decision for the faith without wanting to disturb anything that is public, and that has generated a stance of social action that is *awkwardly* ambivalent about the embrace of public culture, the correction of public culture, and the critical rejection of public culture. The *awkwardness* that besets our common faith, I submit, is an awkwardness of not being sure or clear about how to assess our modern culture, of which we are commonly critical but in which we are commonly embedded to our great benefit. It is an astonishment that much that passes for evangelism is deeply committed to the most destructive forms of privatized individualism, and much that passes for social action appeals precisely to the thinnest forms of liberal rationalism.

This is our common history and we are all, liberals and conservatives, products of it. There seems to me, moreover, little useful gain in interactive polemics and accusations, when we might do well to ponder our common criticism and our common embeddedness in benefits.

It is the case, moreover, that this curious history of church and modernity consists in a web of complex issue that includes both *intellectual* and *economic* matters. Rather than disputing about "evangelism" and "social action"—as large summary slogans—we would do better to rethink *intellectual-epistemological* issues and the ambivalence we all share about gospel scandal and Western rationalism that may take the form of emotive romanticism in a church that does not intend to be obscurantist. In parallel fashion there is an urgent need to rethink *economic* issues wherein market-driven individualism has become the ideological excuse for corporate conformism, wherein conservatives innocently guzzle Coca-Cola and liberals without embarrassment are all dressed up by Nike. The needed rethinking is more serious than are our twin slogans in tension.

As a Scripture teacher, moreover, all of this touches upon historical criticism that began as an intellectual revolution and now functions in many quarters as a resistance to revolution. Thus it is important in the rise of historical criticism—which is Scripture's bow to modernity—to know our own history. Even Methodists would do well to know about the gargantuan misreading of Calvin at Princeton Seminary for over a century, whereby Princeton Seminary became the great fount of fundamentalism.[4] That fundamentalism based on misreading has long since ceased to be theologically serious, but has become instead a loud, thin legitimation for military capitalism. In the late nineteenth century it was the merit of

Charles Briggs to expose the misreading of Calvin, and in the early twentieth century it was Harry Emerson Fosdick who dramatically championed modernity, not because he was an irresponsible liberal, but because he insisted that the gospel should be related to life.

These are hard-won battles for the reliability and viability of the church. And in our latter day, the same issues surface with the Institute of Democracy and Religion that funds a phony Christian advocacy that seems interested in neither the real problems present in our society nor in the claims of the gospel. We do not need to agree on such matters in the present tense, but we have important work to do and theological students must be engaged in it. It is my urging that theological students, and the church more generally, must leave off arguing about labels. In my judgment the church needs *serious conservatives* who are about the evangel as the offer of a new world and *serious liberals* who care deeply about the transformation of society, serious folk who have gifts to give one another and serious gifts to receive from one another as we commonly, in generosity and in good faith, work our way beyond the irrelevant categories and misleading tensions of modernity.

Now needed are pastors and theologians who are willing to read carefully and think deeply about the crisis of our society. The quarrels fostered by modernity do not seem to me very important, and I am suspicious of energy used on them. The truth of the matter is that we now face a newer, deeper crisis. Not only have old Christian codes become tame, easy, and familiar, but the old codes of market individualism also no longer pertain in any concrete way. For the truth is that Western culture as we have counted on it is in a serious state of collapse, a state of collapse that is immediate and concrete for every pastor, even if it is given other names. Specifically *old modes of power, old patterns of certitude*—liberal and conservative—and *old claims of privilege* on which we commonly count are in deep jeopardy. In place of such power, certitude, and privilege, God is doing a new thing, the shape of which we cannot yet see. And not seeing makes us anxious, and then greedy, and then brutal.

As some of you may know, I have suggested that given Old Testament options, the closest analogue we have for our time and place is the coming of exile with the loss of Jerusalem and all it embodied and signified.[5] Ours is a like loss, concrete and political, religious and symbolic, wherein the old, white, male privilege of the West is gone, and we are in a season of displacement and wilderness. If we take the analogue further, it is Israel's theological insistence that the destruction of Jerusalem was not an accident and was not caused by Communists or Moslems or homosexuals, but was done by God, whose patience had been exhausted.

Given this analogue, rough as it is, it offers us fresh access to some important textual resources through which to reread our time and place. When we think displacement and exile in the Old Testament, we are soon drawn to 2 Isaiah, the great evangelist of the Old Testament. It is this poet who found new utterance for God's new way, who intentionally used the word *baśar*—"gospel"—evangel for a message to a people in despair:

> Get you up to a high mountain,
>   O Zion, herald of *good tidings;*
> lift up your voice with strength,
>   O Jerusalem, herald of *good tidings,*
>   lift it up, do not fear;
> say to the cities of Judah,
>   "Here is your God!" (Isa. 40:9, emphasis mine)
> How beautiful upon the mountains
>   are the feet of the messenger who announces peace,
> who brings *good news,*
>   who announces salvation,
>   who says to Zion, "Your God reigns."
>   (Isa. 52:7, emphasis mine)

The evangel intends that the news of God's fresh initiative should break the despair and shatter the ideological grip of the empire so as to free Jews for free, subversive, self-confident activity of a new kind, powered by a peculiar, celebrated identity. Exile evokes gospel![6]

As you know, *exile* is followed by something of a *homecoming* (obscure as it is), in which the restoration and rehabilitation of the community was a heavy task. As you know, moreover, 2 Isaiah as gospel to exiles is intimately linked to the poetry of 3 Isaiah, who had the more difficult task of imagining social reconstruction. What 2 Isaiah is to evangelism, so 3 Isaiah is to social action, for 3 Isaiah imagines around the great public questions of the day, of which I will cite two.

First, the problem of *inclusion or exclusion.* Nervous people exclude. In the church . . . exclude homosexuals. In the civil community . . . exclude undocumented workers and other threatening outsiders. Exclude and make it safe for us. Thus after exile, there is in the Jewish community a drive for exclusiveness and purity . . . only Jews, only pure Jews, only Jews like us. And then comes Isaiah 56:

> To the eunuchs who keep my sabbaths,
>   who choose the things that please me
>   and hold fast my covenant,
> I will give, in my house and within my walls,
>   a monument and a name
>   better than sons and daughters;
> I will give them an everlasting name
>   that shall not be cut off.
> And the foreigners who join themselves to the LORD
>   to minister to him, to love the name of the LORD,

> and to be his servants,
>   all who keep the sabbath, and do not profane it,
>   and hold fast my covenant—
>   these I will bring to my holy mountain,
>   and make them joyful in my house of prayer . . .
>   Thus says the Lord GOD,
>   who gathers the outcasts of Israel,
>   I will gather others to them,
>   besides those already gathered. (vv. 4-8)

The God who gathers intends a community that gathers.

Second, the problem of *linking right worship to right public ethics.* And so we get great attention to worship by people not as gifted or sensitive as Don Saliers. This poet insists that worship is not intended to be narcissistic self-indulgence, but it is visible devotion to the causes of God:

> Is not this the fast that I choose;
>   to loose the bonds of injustice,
>   to undo the thongs of the yoke,
> to let the oppressed go free,
>   and to break every yoke?
> Is it not to share your bread with the hungry,
>   and bring the homeless poor into your house;
> when see the naked, to cover them,
>   and not to hide yourself from your own kin?
>   (Isa. 58:6-7)

I am sure some said, "I thought the subject was worship." And then this poet surely answered, "It is . . . let's fast!"

Later, 3 Isaiah knows about the Priestly tradition, the important claims of in-house holiness. He understands, in the tradition of Leviticus, all about pure everything. But he comes finally to Leviticus 25 and the Jubilee, the most subversive social action ever imagined. And so he holds this part of Leviticus up to the community and says:

> The spirit of the Lord GOD is upon me,
>   because the LORD has anointed me;
> he has sent me to bring good news to the oppressed,
>   to bind up the brokenhearted,
> to proclaim liberty to the captives,
>   and release to the prisoners;
> to proclaim the year of the LORD's favor,
>   and the day of vengeance of our God. (Isa. 61:1-2)

And as you know, this text became the launching text in the evangel of Luke in Luke 4:18-19:

> The Spirit of the Lord is upon me,
>> because he has anointed me to bring good news to the poor.
> He has sent me to proclaim release to the captives
>> and recovery of sight to the blind,
>>> to let the oppressed go free,
> to proclaim the year of the Lord's favor.

The evangel turns out to be a gospel of deep public transformation, deep enough that the authorities sought to kill him.

These are the issues on our plate. No either/or will do, because the church is now summoned to go, intellectually, economically, where no man or woman has ever been before. There is, moreover, a haunting awareness of this in the church. I suspect the haunting includes (a) "Lead me theologically," but also (b) "I dread going." No use for conservatives to pretend the city is not in ruins. No use for liberals to pretend a rebuilding can just be done. We are at more elemental issues that depend on people like us in response to the evangel.

IV

The insistence of gospel-rooted social action is a dream of a genuinely covenantal community of neighbors. That finally is what the "kingdom of God" means. But covenantal neighborliness is a demanding alternative in the world, one deeply at odds with our conventional ways of thought and life. I submit that our work is to bring every aspect of our life together under the neighborliness of God.

In doing so, I dare suggest, there are only two difficult questions. One is *sex*. Sexuality has to do with intimacy and power; the Bible, so it seems to me, intends covenanted sex and *not promiscuity or exploitation*. The other hard question is *money*, for money is about freedom and control, and the Bible is for covenantal economics that are *not promiscuous or exploitative*. It strikes me as odd—but predictable—that conservatives, people who tend to stress evangelism, care a lot about covenantal sexuality but seem strangely naive about promiscuous, self-indulgent economics. Conversely, liberals, those who seem to care about social action, have some sure sense of covenantal economics but tend to mumble about sexuality. Why not a recognition that money and sexuality are twin manifestations of our lust for power, our refusal of commitment, our will to live otherwise, but also our chance for genuine neighborliness as intended by God? I cannot think of a reason to choose up sides on these issues, for such choosing is silly and obsolete.

V

Conclusion: Taylor Branch reports of Martin Luther King Jr.:

> The limitless potential of a young King free to think anything, and therefore to be anything, was constricted by realities that paralyzed and defined him. King buried his face in his hands at the kitchen table. He admitted to himself that he was afraid, that he had nothing left, that the people would falter if they looked to him for strength. Then he said as much out loud. He spoke the name of no deity, but his doubts spilled out as a prayer, ending, "I've come to the point where I can't face it alone." As he spoke these words, the fears suddenly began to melt away. He became intensely aware of what he called an "inner voice" telling him to do what he thought was right. Such simplicity worked miracles, bringing a shudder of relief and the courage to face anything. It was for King the first transcendent religious experience of his life . . . the moment awakened and confirmed his belief that the essence of religion was not a grand metaphysical idea but something personal, grounded in experience—something that opened up mysteriously beyond the predicaments of human beings in their frailest and noblest moments.[7]

The kitchen was the venue for a moment of the evangel. King was claimed in that moment and radically redefined. And then he moved into all the dangerous questions he could discern, not only race but war. The *kitchen* provided the power for the *movement*.

Imagine if he had so prized the evangel that he stayed forever in the kitchen: *no movement!* Or imagine if King had so prized the movement that he had not paused long enough in vulnerability to be reshaped and empowered in the kitchen: *no durable courage or freedom!* It is not an either/or. It is both/and . . . the deep claiming good news and the insistent dangerous public obedience. We need to quit the quarrels, end the silly slogans, and move away from the tired categories given us by modernity. God is doing something new: do you not perceive it!?

4

Reading as Wounded and as Haunted

Our topic of "suspicion" or "trust" is not, cannot be, the first thing. It is always a second thing, always a response to what is already there. Thus I shall begin with *canon* and then consider in turn the reality of suspicion and the possibility of retrieval.

1

Two things are evident about canon. (1) The canon of the Old Testament is a serious attempt to provide a baseline of normalcy that was accomplished by serious believers. (2) The canon is an ideological act that establishes exclusive interests as claims of faith. The problem in coming to terms with the canon is how to relate these two awarenesses that are, in principle, in profound tension with each other.

The canon is an act of bold, venturesome *imagination* that is concerned to ground and sustain a peculiar community. Without lingering over the rich complexity of the prehistory and the literary-theological antecedents of the canon of the Old Testament in the history of Israelite religion, it surely must be recognized that the Old Testament is a statement of social construction, and therefore theological construction, that is immense in its power and in its scope and in its construal of reality.[1] Begging all historical questions, the Torah as primal canon proposes a world rooted at the dawn of order (creation) that culminates in eager longing at the Jordan, about to enter the land of well-being. That is the primal canon that we may take, for our initial purpose, as the normative one.

I mention only two factors that may be pertinent for our reflection. First, that canonical offer of reality is deeply and insistently focused upon Yahweh as the primal agent, but a Yahweh whose character is far from settled. Second, the story of the Torah canon, as James Sanders has seen so well, ends in eager longing, short of promises kept, short of land entered, thus at the outset offering a Yahweh short of fulfillment.[2] The situation of Israel, at the conclusion of the Torah, is anticipatory of the saints in Heb. 11:

> All of those died in faith without having received the promises, but from a distance they saw and greeted them. (v. 13)

The canon, I assume, is essentially *constructive,v* whatever literary or historical antecedents there may be. And if the canon is constructive, then following Peter Berger and Thomas Luckmann, we may take this awesome imaginative act as constitutive in two senses.[3] First, every social construction is a *theodicy*, a justification for who has and does not have, who is in and who is not, who gets and who does not.[4] This theodicy characteristically endorses Jacob rather than Esau, Israelites rather than Canaanites, and Levites rather than Aaronides. And a score of other such exclusions can be noticed. Second, this construction of theodicy surely has an intentional social function, namely, to tease out, authorize, and maintain a certain sociotheological identity for the community and its members, an identity urgent in every time, but especially so in times of crisis. We may suggest, moreover, that such an identity is in contrast to other social identities, so that we may suggest that the canon is in the interest of a "contrast society," an instrument for resistance to other identities, and an affirmation of the identity peculiarly given here.[5]

Because the canon is not of whole cloth but is made into a whole by disparate, disjointed pieces, it seems clear that the canon itself is an invitation to the ongoing process of *interpretation*. That is, the canon does not intend to be a flat, closed, one-dimensional absolute, but rather a field of anticipation in which the norming community continues to adjudicate and interpret between the several pieces that do not obviously or in a single way fit together. I suggest four sorts of evidence that indicate the legitimate expectation of interpretive activity. First, the various disjunctions, repetitions, duplications, and contradictions that are evident—that became the grist for Wellhausen's documentary hypothesis—require interpretation, for no enduring claims are offered about how texts are related to each other. But because this is a norming offer of identity, the text requires more than an *a seriatim* approach, and that "more than" is a daring interpretive judgment. Second, the authorization of Moses as mediator (Exod. 20:18-21) suggests, as Hans-Joachim Kraus and many others have suggested, Israel must have an interpretive office precisely for the work of interpretation that keeps doing the authorized and authorizing work of interpretation.[6] Third, as especially Gerhard von Rad has seen, Deuteronomy—the crucial hinge of canonization—is a tradition that offers a dynamic hermeneutic, whereby nothing can be added to Torah, though the "nothing added" goes on for chapters and chapters, seeking to make the old contemporary (see Deut. 5:3).[7] Fourth, in a very different way, the canons of prophets and writings evidence continuing interpretive authority, whereby, as Gerald Sheppard has shown, canon is transposed eventually into a scribal activity.[8] While the interpretive process is not completely indeterminate, it is clear that it is hugely open and no perspective of closure is permitted a final say.

> But of course, the imaginative and interpretive aspects of canon inescapably invite a recognition of its ideological dimension. Current interest devoted to an ideological critique of canon moves from the recognition that this social construction of reality is not disinterested or neutral or innocuous, but is heavily laden with vested interest of a most exploitative kind. Speaking generically of canon,

I will appeal especially to a discussion found in the work of Charles Altieri. He quotes Frank Kermode: Canons are essentially strategic constructs by which societies maintain their own interests, since the canon allows control over the texts a culture takes seriously and over the methods of interpretation that establish the meaning of "serious."[9]

Altieri concludes in his own comment:

Canons are simply ideological banners for social groups: social groups propose them as forms of self-definition and engage other proponents to test limitations while exposing the contradictions and incapacities of competing groups. . . . When canons are at stake, purposes determine what counts as facts, rather than facts determining the relevant values.[10]

Thus canon is indeed a tool of ideological imposition.

At the outset of our discussion, however, it is important to take into account Altieri's acknowledgment that some things can also be said positively about canon. He identifies two functions of canon. First, canons are *curatorial*: "Canons preserve rich complex contrastive frameworks, which create what I call a cultural grammar for interpreting experience."[11] Second, canons are *normative*: "Canons play the role of institutionalizing idealization: they provide contexts for their own development by establishing examples of what ideals can be, how people have used them as stimuli and contexts for their own self-creation, and why one can claim that present acts can address more than the present."[12]

Altieri accepts Harold Bloom's characteristic suggestion of canon as an instrument for struggle: "Canons make us want to struggle, and they give us the common questions and interests we need to ennoble that project."[13]

Finally, following Northrup Frye: "Canons contribute to something like alternative society within the existing social order. This claim is the ultimate payoff for insisting that our acts of forming and using canons are not reducible to interests—needs and desires—that can be fully explained simply in terms of a specific historical and ideological context."[14]

Speaking more specifically of the canon of Hebrew Scripture, Regina Schwartz, in a remarkable book, shows how the canon traffics in special interests of a brutalizing kind, concerning class, gender, and tribe, as a platform for pervasive violence: "The biblical canon, that is, should not be understood as the product of a peaceful consensus, but as the result of protracted struggles for authority between competing communities."[15] But on the very next page, quoting Harry Gamble with approval, Schwartz agrees that "canon understood as process valorizes biblical pluralism."[16] And even concerning her key substantive argument connecting monotheism and scarcity, she allows:

[t]hese narratives do offer glimpses of another kind of deity, a God of plenitude, of generosity, one who need not protect his turf because it is infinite. And this vision of One, as plenitude, not as particular, would have made exclusive monotheism wither if it could have been sustained. Israel would have longed to be not only a kingdom of prophets or priests, but a kingdom of Gods. Apparently the vision was difficult to sustain.[17]

Thus concerning my first point, I wish to conclude:
1. Canon that "was always there" is a communal baseline; and
2. Canon is an ambiguous phenomenon, saturated with partisan interest, yet inviting to alternative.

II

Suspicion is a response to canon that pays singular attention to the partisan, distorting, ideological work of canon, a dimension of canon now widely recognized among Scripture scholars.[18] Most generically, I suppose, *suspicion* as an interpretive posture is the insistence that the partisan imposition of interest as an offer of objective, reliable reality needs to be exposed for what it is, and not falsely accepted for what it purports to be.

The whole notion of a "hermeneutic of suspicion," as I understand it, comes to us by way of Paul Ricoeur with his appreciation of Marx, Nietzsche, and Freud as "masters of suspicion." It is worth calling attention to two features of Ricoeur's argument that strike me as peculiarly important for our discussion. First, Ricoeur understands that these "three masters of suspicion" were not only "three great destroyers" (which they were):

> It is beyond destruction that the question is posed as to what thought, reason, and even faith still signify. All three clear the horizon for a more authentic word, for a new reign of Truth, not only by means of a "destructive" critique, but by the invention of an art of *interpreting*.[19]

That is, their suspicion is not terminal, but it is instrumental, and needs to be understood dialectically, making way for the new that can only come in the wake of suspicion.

Second, it is important, I submit, that the three masters of suspicion, in Ricoeur's understanding, are concerned with the "illusions of consciousness," especially apparent in the modern world, that is, the world of imagined objectivity and positivism.[20] That is, Marx, Nietzsche, and Freud are concerned with the wholesale cover-up in the nineteenth century. It is at least worth noting that John Murray Cuddihy has argued that Marx, Freud, and Lévi-Strauss are elementally concerned with the cover-up and repression of *Jewishness*, from which is extrapolated a larger notion of cultural denial and repression.[21]

Now the reason I cite this focus of Ricoeur, and derivatively of Cuddihy, is that the "ideology critique" of Hebrew Scripture has reapplied Ricoeur's suspicion in ways that are not so simple or obvious, precisely because the Old Testament canon does not offer such a seamless "Truth" as does modernity, at least not until the hegemonic church has done its triumphalist reading. By seeing that suspicion of the Bible is not quite equivalent to the suspicion of modernity that Ricoeur first targeted, I want to make what I think is an important distinction about suspicion concerning the Bible.

I think it is possible to distinguish between two modes of suspicion in relation to the Bible. The first of these I would call *bodily suspicion,* by which I refer to critique that comes from and gains authority from people who have been hurt by the biases of canon in ways that bespeak genuine injustice and exploitation. The best examples I know are offered by Regina Schwartz, who makes the argument that the *myth of scarcity* (derived from monotheism) makes the claim that there is not "enough," because there is only one God. And because there is not enough, social power, social authority, and social goods must be limited, unshared, and monopolized. Schwartz traces the Bible in this regard in terms of class analysis, gender analysis, and tribal analysis in order to show how the Bible has authorized destructive social policy and antineighborly relationships. By speaking of this as bodily suspicion, I mean criticism that *arises out of pain* and necessitates *verbal candor* that asserts: "A text that causes such hurt cannot be right, cannot be trusted, cannot be revelation!"

The myth of scarcity has authorized the abuse of the poor, the exclusion of women, and the violence of the tribe. The recipients of abuse, exclusion, and violence are, not surprisingly, suspicious and are able to see that the claims made in the name of God are partisan levers of special interest and not more than that. Such suspicion must be taken most seriously.

The other practice of suspicion I will term *idealistic suspicion,* by which I mean it is essentially a critique of "bad ideas" that are not, in the first instance, connected to *bodily damage.* There is currently in Old Testament studies a positivistic suspicion of the theological claims of the Old Testament that appears to me to be the outcome of Enlightenment autonomy. In principle the God-assumptions of the Old Testament are not granted, because no sophisticated person could possibly imagine *holy Agency* in the midst of *human processes,* a claim surely ludicrous on Enlightenment assumptions.

But of course the rejection of these primal theological claims means, in my judgment, that there can be no serious access to the literature at all, leave alone assenting access. This is indeed "unbelief seeking understanding." It is entirely possible that the adrenaline evident in this critique is a response to an earlier, experienced parental authoritarianism in the name of the Bible, so that the wound is not simply intellectual affront but experienced and remembered "bodily" pain. That is, *the intellectual rejection is simply a covert way to protest the bodily pain.* If that be the taproot of such intellectual suspicion, then it must be honored. But before it can be honored, it must be named for what it is and not treated under false labels. Alternatively, if the intellectual rejection is not rooted in bodily pain but is only intellectual, then the work of suspicion needs to be dialectical, not only Enlightenment suspicion of the Bible that is "obscurantist," but biblical suspicion of Enlightenment that is in some important measure an illusion.

III

Only now do we come to the assigned topic, "Trust or Suspicion," the latter term being a translation of Paul Ricoeur's rubric of "retrieval." Retrieval is the capacity to pay trustful attention to these texts after we have suspiciously noticed their ideological, hurtful propensity. Thus the sequence to be considered is:

> *canon—suspicion—retrieval* as a grid for interpretation. It has been otherwise also phrased as, first naïveté . . . critique . . . second naïveté;[22] precritical . . . .critical . . . postcritical; or orientation . . . disorientation . . . new orientation.[23]

In all of these formulations, the first move into criticism (suspicion) is readily made in our common work. But the second move into retrieval is the one in question. I propose to consider this more demanding move first theoretically, and then to take up two texts as case studies in retrieval.

It is important to recognize that in his initial formulation of the matter, Paul Ricoeur understood suspicion and retrieval to be dialectically related, for it is in the character of a "classic" not to be defeated by suspicion, but only to generate a fresh, considerably altered reading when the wound of ideology is exposed. Indeed, if a text is defeated by such suspicion, then it likely is not a classic and surely would not, in Christian parlance, be taken as "God's word." It is clear, among other things from our being here together, that the Bible has not yet been defeated by such suspicion.

David Tracy, who closely follows Ricoeur but is much more pointedly theological and in the end is interested in the Bible as "classic," understands the interpreter as one who stands always in a community of tradition, one

> formed by the community and as responsible to the wider community of inquirers and readers, the subject is communal. . . . Every present moment is, in fact, formed by both the memories of the tradition and the hopes, desires, critical demands for transformation for the future. The notion of the present moment as pure instant, as

ever-receding image, is as mistaken as the allied notion of a pure—isolated, purely autonomous—subject.

> The subject as interpreter may despise the tradition as a dead-ening force, a bourgeois humanist hoax, an obscurantist fraud, a poisonous creature of *ressentiment*. But the interpreter must still interpret that tradition in the hope, and with the ethical demand, of exposing its fraudulence, suspecting its claims, denouncing its injustice. . . .
> Then the second moment of interpretation begins. If the classic is a classic, to repeat, another force comes into play. That force is the claim to attention, a vexing, a provocation exerted on the subject by the classic text. . . . My *doxai* are suddenly confronted with a *para-doxon* demanding attention. My finite status as this historical sub-ject is now confronted with the classic and its claim upon me. . . . It happens, it demands, it provokes . . . the dialogue will demand that the interpreter concentrate, above all, on the subject matter of the text: the questions, responses, hints, resonances, feelings—the "world." . . . The dialogue will demand that the interpreter enter into the back-and-forth movement of that disclosure in the dialec-tics of self-transcending freedom, released by the text upon a finite, historical, dialogical reader and received by the text from a now dialoguing reader.[24]

While Tracy's rhetoric may be a bit dense, in my judgment, he is surely correct. It is that grounded in the community of the text, we are not finished with the text with our best suspicion, because the community of interpreta-tion in which we are irreversibly rooted continues to be haunted by the text and its insistences. This is surely true of those with *bodily pain* caused by the text who perforce in hope keep turning to the wounding text for ways in which it may be a healing text. Very differently, it is even true of the *intel-lectual rejecters* of the text who, even in their Enlightenment dismissiveness, never walk away from the text, if for no other reason than to assault it one more time, ironically perhaps like Jacob, still anticipating a blessing from the text.

I do not know why this claim in the text persists beyond suspicion. It could be that suspicion is enough to end the matter, and here and there it might. Our concern here, "Suspicion or Trust," is the question of *ending* with suspicion or *going on* to retrieval whereby affirmation is the end of the matter, by which I mean a large prerational propensity to attentiveness and rage, a prerational propensity that in the end may be a gift of the Spirit—that is, the willingness and ability to stay with a text that so manifestly wounds is not explained rationally but in the inscrutability that the faithful name as spirit.

By the same token, I find Ricoeur's (and Tracy's) suspicion-retrieval par-alleled in Michael Buckley's dialectic of theism-atheism. In the end, it is

Hegel's "contradiction" between theism and atheism (or in our terms, suspicion and retrieval) that is generative of interpretation. So Buckley avers:

> Contradiction does not threaten ideas, but it suggests unrealized potentiality, the inadequacy of a present formulation, or the becoming which is their actual form of being.[25]
>
>   It was critical to recognize that "atheism" [for us "suspicion"] was parasitic. The word, its significance, and its application were derived from what was denied. . . . The meaning of atheism, then, is always dialectical, that is, it emerges from its contradiction.[26]

If I understand Buckley rightly (and his work is dense), it is that atheism arises with the Enlightenment because religion tried to justify itself in categories essentially alien to its claims:

> Atheism is not the secret of religion, as Feuerbach would have it, but it is the secret contradiction within a religion that denies its own abilities to deal cognitively with what is central to its nature. Atheism is the secret of that religious reflection which justifies the sacred and its access to the sacred primarily through its own transmogrification into another form of human knowledge or practice, as though the only alternative to fideism were such an alienation, as though religion had to become philosophy to remain religion. The unique character of religious knowledge does not survive this reduction.[27]

In my judgment suspicion characteristically arises when a demand is made—a demand characteristic of Western hegemonic Christendom—to justify and appropriate the text in ways alien to the text, that is, to conform the text to rational triumphalism and western modes of reading that override the very disjunctiveness of Jewish discourse on faith, upon which the claims ride. Buckley quotes Julius Guttmann:

> [Israel's] idea of God, [is] not the fruit of philosophic speculation but the product of the immediacy of the religious consciousness. . . . The decisive feature of monotheism is that it is not grounded in an abstract idea of God, but in an intensely powerful divine will which rules history. This ethical voluntarism implies a thoroughly personalistic conception of God, and determines the specific character of the relationship between God and man.[28]

Retrieval then consists of (1) facing honestly the *wounding* caused by the text (which may be expressed in modes of dismissive rationalism) and (2) the readiness to continue to be *haunted* by the wounding text in the affectively grounded expectation that there is more here than wounding but also healing.

    Thus Israel can hear God say of God (and we say also of the text):

> See now that I, even I, am he;
> there is no god beside me.

I kill and I make alive;
I wound and I heal;
and no one can deliver from my hand. (Deut. 32:39)
Come, let us return to the LORD;
for it is he who has torn, and he will heal us;
he has struck down, and he will bind us up. (Hosea 6:1)
I form light and create darkness,
I make weal and create woe;
I the LORD do all these things. (Isa. 45:7)

These statements, clearly true of the God of the Bible, do not surprise us. They do not yield what Luther called "a theology of glory," but instead invite to life in the contradiction. Trust in these texts is trust in the midst of contradictions that have holy rootage but that generate scandal in the daily practice of our bodily life.

IV

I want now to consider in turn two texts that I take up with no assurance that I can "manage," but to think with you and in front of you of the demands of our topic. First, I refer to 1 Samuel 15, the narrative in which Saul is dismissed from kingship by Samuel because he did not practice the commanded extermination (ḥerem) of the Amalekites, an extermination long mandated in Exod. 17:14-16 and Deut. 25:17-19 and here championed by Samuel. The mandate in the narrative is voiced by Samuel at the outset:

Thus says the LORD of hosts, "I will punish the Amalekites for what they did in opposing the Israelites when they came up out of Egypt. Now go and attack Amalek, and utterly destroy all that they have; do not spare them, but kill both man and woman, child and infant, ox and sheep, camel and donkey." (vv. 2-3)

Saul does not exterminate the Amalekite king Agag nor the best of the valuable livestock, a clear violation of Samuel's ruthless command. The reason for the violation is not clear. Perhaps he is prudent to save good property; we are not told that he is a compassionate "softie." He says only that he enacted the mandate of the people whom he heeded.

It is not difficult to be "suspicious" of this text, for the ruthless mandate is rooted in old, we would think, irrelevant dreams of ethnic cleansing, now advocated by a crusty, tough leader who seems only to guard his power. Saul is vigorously condemned and rejected for not killing!

Our suspicion is that the driving force of the narrative is either ignoble ethnic claims or the ideological self-justification of Samuel. Either way, we can imagine that Saul is the better figure who is done in. If we go behind Saul, moreover, we arrive at Yahweh, who commands but who is not very winsome. So we conclude that this is hardly a compelling biblical ethic, one too often replicated in the twentieth century. We may in general agree with the dictum of v. 22—"To obey is better than sacrifice"—but surely not this obedience.

But how do we engage in retrieval? How do we take this text seriously as a *religious* text? I suggest three lines of approach, none of which denies the force of the suspicion at which we have arrived. First, the term *ḥerem* that dominates the text is in the presence of two other quite conspicuous terms. The term *ḥamal*—spare, have compassion—is used three times:

- as negative mandate: "Do not spare them" (v. 3);
- as report: "Saul and the people spared Agag and the best . . . " (v. 9);
- as justification: "the people spared the best" (v. 15).

The narrative is fully aware that "having compassion" is a genuine alternative to *ḥerem,* or from an ideological perspective, a genuine seduction. The term *ḥamal* is placed in the narrative as a clear protest against *ḥerem.*

The term *ḥesed*—steadfast love—is used only once, in v. 6, to celebrate the Kenites, who are friends, in contrast with the deep enmity felt toward the Amalekites. I submit that when *ḥerem* is placed with *ḥamal* and *ḥesed,* the narrative skillfully demonstrates that it knows about preferable alternatives to *ḥerem* that expose *ḥerem* as an extreme option. And while the ideologue Samuel may desire ethnic cleansing, Saul knows more, and the God hovering in the midst of this text also knows better, perhaps not yet free for *ḥesed* and *ḥamal,* perhaps not yet powerful enough against the spokesperson with whom Yahweh is stuck. From now on, *ḥerem* must be heard in the protesting company of *ḥamal* and *ḥesed.*

Second, as is often noticed, the term *niham* is used three times in this text:

- I regret that I made Saul king, for he has turned back from following me (v. 11).
- Moreover the Glory of Israel will not recant or change his mind; for he is not a mortal, that he should change his mind (v. 29).
- The Lord was sorry that he had made Saul king over Israel (v. 35).

The renderings in the NRSV are "regret, recant, sorry." Two things are to be observed. First, the usage in vv. 10 and 35 asserts that Yahweh is regretful about Saul, but v. 29, alternatively, asserts that Yahweh will not recant or change his mind. The three uses together suggest that Yahweh is seen here as a problematic character, not as stable or one-dimensional as suggested in the harsh ideology of Samuel. Thus the God who authorizes *ḥerem* is not flatly certain, but is seen to host some openness.

Moreover, the term used three times, *nahûm,* is in each instance taken to mean to "change mind" or "reverse judgment." One of these uses is a *pi'el* intensive verb form and two are *niph'al* reflexive form. The renderings are likely correct. It is, in my judgment, important to recognize that the same root word, especially in 2 Isaiah, means "comfort" (40:1; 49:13; 51:3). I do not suggest that "comfort" is the intent of the term here. It is plausible, nonetheless, to imagine that the narrator and the hearers of the text would hear hints and traces of "comfort" in this brutal narrative. There is a God of comfort present here who may indeed move past *ḥerem* to *ḥamal* and *ḥesed*. Who knows what is heard or what is meant to be heard?[29]

Yet a third observation is pertinent. Saul does not destroy the Amalekites and is therefore condemned by Samuel. Moreover, Saul twice confesses, "I have sinned" (vv. 24, 30). But he will not be forgiven. Every listener to this text in Israel knows that this larger narrative is rushing on to David, "a neighbor of yours who is better than you" (v. 28). When we arrive in the narrative at David, two things strike us. First, after the murder of Uriah, when David is confronted by Nathan, the king says to the prophet, "I have sinned" (2 Sam. 12:13), whereupon he is promptly forgiven. Simply put, Saul is condemned for not killing; David is forgiven for killing! Moreover, in 1 Samuel 30, David is at war with the Amalekites. After an initial setback, David is triumphant over them. We are told:

> David recovered all that the Amalekites had taken; and David rescued his two wives. Nothing was missing, whether small or great, sons or daughters, spoil or anything that had been taken; David brought back everything. David also captured all the flocks and herds, which were driven ahead of the other cattle; people said, "This is David's spoil." (vv. 18-20)

The remainder of the narrative concerns the distribution of the "spoil" (vv. 20-21). The contrast between Saul and David in these narratives is stunning. Retrieval might suggest (1) that the harshness of 1 Samuel 15 is not the sustainable harshness of Yahweh, but the quixotic way of Samuel, for the God of the narrative (or at least the narrator) knows about compassion and steadfast love, or (2) at least the old dictums do not pertain forever. Given time and a new cast of characters, brutality is slowly reconfigured.

What is to be noticed, I suggest, is that the text that wounds in *ḥerem* is a text that has on its horizon certainly *ḥamal* and *ḥesed*, and perhaps "comfort" as well. The text invites dialogue to see whether things are unsettled and open; if they are unsettled and open, the text permits a rereading in the context of a God who spares later Amalekites, who later still "comforts" Israel, and who later yet is known to be a "God of all comfort" (2 Cor. 1:3, as in RSV).

V

The second text I consider is Psalm 89. In vv. 1-37, this psalm is a liturgical celebration of the Davidic dynasty and the sure promises made to that dynasty by Yahweh:

I have found my servant David;
    with my holy oil I have anointed him;
my hand shall always remain with him;
    my arm shall also strengthen him. . . .
My faithfulness and *steadfast love* shall be with him;
    and in my name his horn shall be exalted; . . .
Forever I will keep my *steadfast love* for him,
    and my covenant with him will stand firm.
I will establish his line forever,
    and his throne as long as the heavens endure.
If his children forsake my law
    and do not walk according to my ordinances,
if they violate my statutes
    and do not keep my commandments,
then I will punish their transgression with the rod
    and their iniquity with scourges;
but I will not remove from him my *steadfast love*,
    or be false to my faithfulness.
I will not violate my covenant,
    or alter the word that went froth from my lips.
Once for all I have sworn by my holiness;
    I will not lie to David.
His line shall continue forever,
    and his throne endure before me like the sun.
It shall be established forever like the moon,
    an enduring witness in the skies.
          (Ps. 89:20-21, 24, 28-37, emphasis mine)

Yahweh's commitment to David is "once for all," irreversible, to all generations. It may particularly interest us that the term *hesed*—steadfast love—occurs three times in vv. 24, 28, and 33. Indeed, *hesed* becomes a kind of tag word for the dynasty, though even its daring claims are not able to monopolize the term. I take this psalm and its parallel in 2 Samuel 7 to be a bold dynastic claim made in liturgy, saturated with propagandistic intention, but also laden with what must have been Israel's deepest faith conviction. The rhetoric of absolute promise, moreover, is echoed in the evangelical talk of the church concerning God's sure promises to abide in sovereign graciousness.

In terms of generic claims, this text readily invites questions of theodicy, concerning suffering in a world promised fidelity. But of course in ancient Israel matters are never generic. They are concrete and on the ground. So much is acknowledged in vv. 38-51 that surprises us, apparently a lament. The turn of the psalm in v. 38, after v. 37, is abrupt:

But now you have spurned and rejected him;
    you are full of wrath against your anointed.

> You have renounced the covenant with your servant;
> You have defiled his crown in the dust. (vv. 38-39)

The rhetoric is a direct accusation against Yahweh in the form of a vigorous assertion that Yahweh has been inattentive and unfaithful. The following lines reflect the destruction of the city, seeming to require the judgment that this is a complaint about the destruction of Jerusalem and the ensuing exile, when Israel lost everything and the dynasty lost its throne.

The verses echo the characteristic yearning, angry hope of complaint:

> How long, O Lord? Will you hide yourself forever?
> How long will your wrath burn like fire? (v. 46)

In the end, these lines can recall that *hesed* was used three times in the foregoing and now the question must be posed:

> Lord, where is your steadfast love of old,
> which by your faithfulness you swore to David? (v. 49)

The question is an urgent one, not rhetorical. It is here unanswered as it often is in Israel; Israel continues to wait for an answer. The tone of the final verses (vv. 50-51) is not resignation but insistence: "Remember, O Lord!" Israel is not yet driven to despair or silence. On the basis of the old guarantee of *hesed*, Israel prays determinedly in the midst of a failed *hesed*. Israel knows that the God who has promised *hesed* is committed to it and must be held to it, held insistently and uncompromisingly. But for all of that, *hesed is not given*.

By way of retrieval, I make three comments. First, this psalm, given its two parts in close connection, is a meditation upon the crucial nature and lack of resolve of Yahweh's *hesed*. *Hesed* is Yahweh's peculiar forte. It is also Israel's enduring and odd agenda. Israel is promised *hesed* and now completely lacks *hesed*. Its lack is concrete, but it becomes a large God-question, an exilic question about God's fidelity. *Hesed* is the proper and right matter about which Israel and Yahweh must struggle, because it is the identifying quality of this odd relationship. Note well, *hesed* was already a trace in 1 Samuel 15, only mentioned with reference to the Kenites who did not figure in the narrative. But with David, *hesed* is now front and center, as promise and as problem, for the faith of Israel.

But second, inside the psalm, there is no *hesed*. The reason is exile. Exile is Israel's large, defining act of suspicion. Israel will not lie about exile, will not lie to protect Yahweh or to deceive itself. Israel will not lie about its circumstance, its loss, or its pain in order to protect large theological slogans. I stress this because my experience is that many Christians feel obligated somehow to protect God's honor at all costs, including the cost of denial. Not so Israel. Whatever Israel retrieves, it retrieves in the midst of acknowledged wound.

Third, the psalm ends with a doxology in v. 52:

> Blessed be the LORD forever.
> Amen and Amen.

I know, of course, that this brief doxology does not really belong to the psalm; it is an editorial statement to give closure to book 3 of the Psalter that ends here. And yet, it is attached precisely to this psalm. The disjunction between the complaint of vv. 50-51 and the doxology of v. 52 is an exemplar of the dialectic of suspicion and retrieval in the faith of Israel. Without denying loss, Israel is capable of affirmation, an affirmation of what is remembered and what is hoped but also of what is not in hand.

VI

The study of the *ideology of canon* tends to proceed as if the canon were innocent and one-dimensional and is shocked by the practice of suspicion. But such a notion of the "innocence of canon" is a gross reduction that results from the most hegemonic reading. This reading is interested only in flat summaries and pays no attention to the details of anguish, ambiguity, incongruity, and playfulness that are present in the text. That hegemonic reading appears to be a great temptation of Christian readers, perhaps because of the beguilement of Hellenistic philosophy through which we have learned to read, perhaps because of the Constantinian collusion that requires simplicity, or perhaps because of a singular passion for Jesus Christ who resolves everything. Indeed, it is hegemonic reading, I propose, that evokes suspicion, because hegemonic reading is triumphalist and acknowledges no wounding. That practiced denial is noticed most by those who are wounded in the interpreting process and who know, in the exile of their own scars, that the claims are not true.

- It is not true that *ḥerem* is an act of legitimate obedience, for the God of all comfort is already "working the crowd."
- It is not true that Yahweh's *ḥesed* is sure, because exiles do happen.

Suspicion is the insistence, born of wound, that one-dimensional, triumphalist claims—either in the text or in interpretation—are not true and are too expensive in the denials that they require.

But what I most want to insist upon is that the canon of the Old Testament itself contains suspicion as a part of its *canonical claim*. It presents the dialectic of suspicion and retrieval as the *quintessential process,* a process perhaps peculiarly amenable to Jewish modes of discourse but finally rooted in Yahweh's own unsettled holiness. Israel is indeed capable of making large *claims* for Yahweh. But Israel is equally capable of large *assaults* on Yahweh, for not living up to Yahweh's own self-announced claims. It is this process of *claim* and *assault* that constitutes the drama of the canon. That drama is especially evident in the full and rich interplay between *hymns* that voice the claim and *complaints* that deny the claim— an interplay evident in Psalm 89 and everywhere evident in Israel's prayers. The interesting question is not how ancient Israel found the nerve to be face to face in this way with Yahweh; rather it is how we now characteristically find this too awkward, so that we have lied to our detractors, to our children, and to ourselves. Our wounded life requires that suspicion not be antithetical to trust but rather be a serious, proper, and inescapable dimension of good-faith trust.

VII

I end with five parallel conclusions:

1. The canon of the Old Testament understands the *exile* and the laments and complaints that voice exile as the characteristic suspicion of all easy claims made for Yahweh. The exile is the irreducible datum of Israel's life through which all of the claims for Yahweh must be worked. As in Psalm 89, it is clear that the main claims for Yahweh are deeply jeopardized by exile, but Israel will not accommodate its pain to make things easy for Yahweh.

2. The canon of the New Testament understands that *Friday crucifixion* is the characteristic suspicion of all claims made for the gospel of Jesus Christ. It is and remains always a question of how deep we imagine the *caesura* of Friday to go. But it does go deep. It goes very deep. It goes so deep, says Jürgen Moltmann, that on that day, "The Fatherlessness of the Son is matched by the Sonlessness of the Father."[30]

But suspicion is in order, for after the early church had insisted upon "Jesus Christ *and him crucified*," the church has been endlessly busy with a theology of glory that acts as if all the wounds of Friday are easily coun- tered by Easter, when in fact the wounds are not covered but instead live unsettled with continuing healing power.[31] The covering of suspicion in the name of triumph is precisely what cuts us off from the Crucified One and makes us imitators of every trivialization, an imitation deep in our common bones.

3. Contemporary communities of faith—Jewish and Christian—under- stand that the *midcentury holocaust* is the primal act of suspicion against every easy claim made for truth in Western culture. It is not necessary to insist that the Holocaust is unique, though that case can be made. It is enough to see, with Emil Fackenheim, that the Holocaust "cross-examines" all modernity and all of Christianity and all of Judaism that are congruent with modernity.[32] While the Holocaust in its depth and intensity and irra- tionality is more stunning to us, it is of a piece with *exile and crucifixion* in posing questions that our retrievals must not glibly answer.

4. A vignette from a class: in a class just ended in the exegesis of Samuel, there were twenty-two students, three of whom are African American. One of the latter, Bill Bailey, insisted that Samuel in 1 Samuel 15 was the voice of old, nervous, intimidating human power. Most of the white students are more innocently fideistic about the Bible than is Mr. Bailey. They insisted, not yet wise in the ways of suspicion, that Samuel was indeed voicing God's intent, because that is how it is presented in the Bible. That is the voice of God, difficult as it is for us to hear. The give-and-take between students did not move but kept being a reiteration of these two quite different perspectives. The white students pushed the brutality of Samuel upstairs while Mr. Bailey held out for skewed human perception. We found no resolve to the issue except that I raised the question to the class: Is it accidental that it takes an African American, who has lived a while, to be suspicious about God-authorized violence, whereas our whiteness need not notice, having not yet been addressed directly by violence? This was the same Bill Bailey who earlier concluded that in 1 Samuel 5, Dagon's arms were broken because some Israelites sneaked in and pushed over the statue in the night. I observed to Bill that he was a "liberal." He responded, "Maybe so, but they did break the arms!"

5. Claus Westermann has observed that the psalms of lament and complaint in ancient Israel are acts of *protest:*

> Insofar as the absurd is laid before God, the lament of the nation contains a dimension of protest, the protest of a people who cannot understand what has happened or has been done to them. It is a protest directed to God to be sure, but it is nevertheless a protest; it does not endure absurdity submissively and patiently: it protests! The protest itself arises out of the perception of fate as absurd, as for example the enslavement in Egypt; it lays the matter out before God so that he will do something about it. That the lament is heard implies that God has accepted the protest.[33]

In such a context, submissiveness is always premature. It is my judgment that *protest* is indeed theological suspicion, a suspicion that deeply questions easy claims made for God that are contradicted by the evident pain that says otherwise.[34]

Moreover, Westermann has observed that in Christian liturgy and theology, protest is regularly transposed into confession:

> From the standpoint of the Pauline doctrine there can be no lament without a confession of sin; if a lamenter appears before God, he appears as one who is guilty. But the lament is not a constituent part of Christian prayer, and we can say that in a certain sense the confession of sin has become the Christianized form of lament: *Mea culpa, mea culpa, mea maxima culpa!* The result of this is that both in Christian dogmatics and in Christian worship suffering as

opposed to sin has receded far into the background. . . . We must now ask whether Paul and Pauline oriented theology has not understood the work of Christ in a anisette matter. . . . A correction of this sort would have far-reaching consequences. One of these would be that the lament, as the language of suffering, would receive a legitimate place in Christian worship, as it had in the worship of the Old Testament.[35]

I move from suspicion to protest because I want to insist that a hermeneutic of suspicion, in the end, is not a cerebral, cognitive matter. It is rather a deeply existential matter that concerns *woundedness* that cannot be covered over by impervious triumphalism. Israel knew that, and therefore insisted that the reality of suffering-protest-suspicion belongs not only to the life of the faithful, but to the life of God. To see that suspicion and trust are intimately linked as suspicious trust and trustful suspicion is, in my judgment, a recovery of a theology of the cross. It is of this that Paul asserts: "For God's foolishness is wiser than human wisdom, and God's weakness is stronger than human strength" (1 Cor. 1:25).

Suspicion is not an academic act. It is an act of faith to enter into the suffering that gives the lie to theological triumphalism. In such a practice that does not need to protect God and does not fear to enter into the texts that voice protest, we may become more responsible Friday-Sunday people who know about truth and pain, about strength and weakness, about new life out of death. The canon insists upon such a horizon for faith. The God who hides in the canon knows about this horizon of life and is not scandalized by it.

5

Four Indispensable Conversations among Exiles

It is abundantly and unmistakably clear that we are in a deep *dislocation* in our society that touches every aspect of our lives. It is in any case a deep displacement and perhaps a transition, though none of us can yet see the completion of the transition.

- The old certitudes are less certain.
- The old privileges are under powerful challenge.
- The old dominations are increasingly ineffective, and we seem not to be so clearly in charge.
- The old institutions (governmental, educational, judicial, medical) seem less and less to deliver what is intended and long counted upon.
- The old social fabrics of neighborliness are eroded into selfishness, fear, anger, and greed.

I hazard the judgment that these displacements are irreversible. There is, in my judgment, no going back to that, because the circumstances making that world sustainable have gone from us.

It is equally evident that this massive dislocation, about which we all know, touches the church:

- There is great confusion in the church about authority.
- There is bewilderment about mission, for we tend to think in triumphalist categories, even while some speak of the United States as a "mission field."
- We all know about the heavy, mean-spirited disputes about norms and ethics.
- Questions of institutional survival lead to anxiety about membership and growth.
- Budget worries in the church abound.

Because the church has been intimately connected with these old realities of certitude, privilege, and domination, it shares a common jeopardy with other old institutional patterns in the face of such dislocation.

1

Our bewildered, numbed, despairing society lacks ways of thinking and ways of speaking that can give us remedial access to the crisis, that can (1) go deep into the crisis and so avoid *denial,* and (2) imagine past the crisis, and so avoid *despair* enacted as abdicating silence. It is clear to me that the twin temptations of denial and despair are powerfully at work to prevent any serious engagement of the crisis of dislocation into which we are now plunged.

I have been asking about the church and its peculiar role and responsibility in the midst of this dislocation. I propose that the church,

- when it is attentive to its memory;
- when it remembers its ancient miracles that it continues to treasure;
- when it has the courage to speak its own cadences rather than the accents of everyone else's language;
- when it reengages old seasons of hurt that are still poignant in our awareness;
- when it recalls its deep insistences against the Holy One;

that is, when the church accepts its own past life with God, it has ways of speaking and ways of knowing and ways of imagining that could matter in the present cultural dislocation. I propose that the church has available precisely the rhetorical and testimonial antidotes to the current emergency of *denial* and *despair*.

II

An Old Testament teacher, when thinking about *dislocation*, moves by "dynamic analogy" to the *exile*, the determining and defining event of the Old Testament. The community of ancient Israel, by its stubbornness, its refusal to heed the purposes of Yahweh, and its resolve to act against neighborliness, brought upon itself the great crisis of 587 B.C.E. In that year,

- the beloved temple in Jerusalem was destroyed
- the cherished city was burned
- the king was exiled
- the leading citizens were deported and made fugitives
- public life came to an end

For ancient Israel,

- it was the end of privilege
- it was the end of certitude
- it was the end of domination
- it was the end of viable public institutions
- it was the end of a sustaining social fabric

Not to overstate, it was *the end of life* with God, which Israel had taken for granted. In that moment of wrenching, our mothers and fathers in faith learned that even the life guaranteed by God is tenuous and can end. In that staggering moment, ancient Israel faced the temptation of *denial,* the pretense that the loss had not happened, the temptation of *despair,* the refusal and ability to see any way out.

It is my judgment, I think without extravagant overstatement, that our present deep social dislocation is a parallel to that of Israel's ancient exile in depth, intensity, massiveness, and urgency, in which we, like them, are tempted in the same ways to denial and despair.

It is my thought, then, that the *traditions of exile* in the Old Testament—remarkably rich, generative, and imaginative—might be a resource and indeed perhaps the only resource of speech and imagination that can move us *under denial to reality* and *beyond despair into possibility*. Ancient Israel understood that unless the loss is processed in order to penetrate the denial and despair, newness will not come. It is not, I suspect, different among us.

Out of those traditions of exile, I want to suggest *four ways of speech* and *four dimensions of faithful imagination* that the church can offer and practice as antidotes to denial and despair. In thinking this through, however, the offer of such practices of speech and imagination requires among us a refocus of the church, a "back to basics" that recognizes that the church is not a convenience store, or a massage parlor, or a defender of the status quo. It is, as the exiles came reluctantly to face, an *alternative community,* deeply placed in risk, summoned in baptism to a world in which Yahweh, the God of Israel, is a pivotal player. Such an affirmation requires that we church people ourselves be alerted to *the odd identity* to which we are summoned, for without *odd baptismal identity* the church has nothing to offer and is likely to be a feeble echo of the denial and despair so dense around us.

III

The first speech practice I mention that this community of loss and hope knows about is the practice of *honesty, sadness, rage, anger,* and *loss,* That ancient community lost nearly everything when it lost Jerusalem. In like manner, I believe that our current cultural loss is immense, the loss of old, patterns of hegemony that shakes the privilege of whites and males and their various entourages. I believe the consequence of such loss, moreover, is enormous rage, which shows up variously in family abuse, in absurd armament programs and budgets, in abusive prison policies, in passion for capital punishment, and in assaults upon the poor in the name of "reform." All of these, I submit, are displaced practices of anger that predictably end in brutality.

Instead of taking our rage and indignation at loss down that path of brutality, I imagine the church knows from Israel about grief and rage addressed to God, for it is (perhaps) precisely God who is busy terminating privilege and certitude. The model speech practices of ancient Israel that may break denial are the speeches of complaint and lamentation, that dare to say out loud how overwhelming is the loss, how great the anxiety, how deep the consequent fear.

The *sadness* is as in Lam. 1:2:

> She weeps bitterly in the night,
>   with tears on her cheeks;
> among all her lovers,
>   she has no one to comfort her.

The poet brings to speech a bereft, failed Jerusalem. The *rage* in the more familiar words of Ps. 137:9:

> Happy shall they be who take your little ones
>   and dash them against the rocks!

The indignation tilted toward vengeance sounds this way:

> We have become a taunt to our neighbors,
>   mocked and derided by those around us. . . .
> Return sevenfold into the bosom of our neighbors
>   the taunts with which they taunted you, O Lord!
>   (Ps. 79:4, 12)

The poet dares to echo ancient Lamech with his unrestrained thirst for vengeance, seventy times seven. The bitterness sounds like a litany familiar in our society indicting humanists, Muslims, homosexuals, communists, only now it is all addressed to the God from whom no secret can be hidden. The utterance is not merely catharsis, though it is that. It is also a practice of prayer that is honest and courageous. These speech practices offer an opportunity for brutalizing loss to be turned into an act of faith that may in turn issue into positive energy. These speech practices provide a way to do something with our brutalizing rage at loss so that it does not escalate into antineighborly hurt.

IV

The second speech practice about which this ancient community of dismay and disorder knew concerns the disciplines of *order and holiness*. There were those of a sacramental inclination who believed that life in Jerusalem had been cheapened and trivialized and emptied of meaning by commoditization. All parts of life, including God, self, and neighbor, had been reduced to managed "things." It is the sacramental voice of the priests (identified in scholarship as "The Priestly tradition")—a language markedly absent in our shrill moralisms—that insists that in the confusion when old patterns of meaning are destroyed, one may resort to liturgic construals of ordered holiness. Of course people like us shy away from holiness, worried about ostentatiousness or self-righteous punctiliousness. But the priests, in

that urgent situation, do not flinch. They say it right out without embarrassment:

> I am the LORD your God; sanctify yourselves therefore, and be holy,
> for I am holy. You shall not defile yourselves. . . . You shall be holy
> for I am holy. (Lev. 11:44-45)

> You shall be holy, for I the LORD your God am holy. (Lev. 19:2)

> Consecrate yourselves therefore, and be holy; for I am the LORD
> your God. (Lev. 20:7; cf. 20:26; 21:6-8)

In response to the crisis of displacement, Leviticus (and the larger Priestly
tradition) advocates stringent notions of holiness. And indeed, we likely
would not want to follow all of their concreteness abut purity and the
shunning of defilement. What interests me about their urgings, however,
is that these displaced people, for whom almost everything was out of
control, with sacramental imagination undertook to reorder and recover
life by an intentional resolve about *communion with God*. They understood in passionate ways that life in faith is not happenstance or accidental—or automatic. It cannot be presumed upon but requires attentiveness.
The tradition of Leviticus urges disciplines of holiness, concrete bodily
ways whereby life is knowingly directed toward the holiness of God that
comforts even as it demands. This holiness—without which we cannot
live—is not available upon demand but arises in and through practices
that invite and welcome the awesomeness of God to come dwell among
us. Indeed, as the Priestly tradition tells it, the community may and must
prepare a place that is a suitable habitat for God's presence.

The danger and temptation in dislocation is to become self-preoccupied
and self-indulgent. This sacramental tradition knows that at bottom, even
this deep dislocation cannot empty life of the mystery of God, a mystery
that requires concrete actions and sustained thought. I suspect that the
reduction of life to having and possessing, to surface and trivial entertainment, is a sign and measure of our deathly alternative to holiness. Indeed,
in a tradition quite unlike the priests, the prophet Amos warns against such
indulgence that will eventually drive Israel from the land and drive Yahweh
from Israel (Amos 6:4-7).

Leviticus pursues the theme of disciplined holiness on a micro scale, as it
pertains to the daily nature of life. The same people, the priests, go large in
Genesis 1, a text more familiar to us. The creation poem of Gen. 1:1—2:4a
is an exilic liturgy that affirms the goodness of an ordered world under
God's governing blessing. As such it is a counterliturgy, because it affirms
precisely those aspects of life governed by God that seem remote from the
lived reality of these displaced people. In their worship, these folk would
not give in to their circumstance. And for that reason this characterization of the world as God's creation is marked by the reiterated litany-like

verdict, "It is good, it is good, it is good, it is very good." In the end, more-over, it is affirmed, against circumstance: "God blessed the seventh day and hallowed it, because on it God rested from all the work that he had done in creation" (Gen. 2:3).

The beginning point for holiness that recovers and reorders life is indeed *sabbath*—holy time—not legalism and "blue laws," but also not frantic, feverish, self-indulgent entertainment. The priests envision, in heaven as on earth, a restfulness that makes neighborly communication possible, apart from the impositions of production and consumption. Sacramentalism is a cogent alternative to despair, an awareness that even here and even now, God's demanding and assuring presence pertains.

V

The third speech practice that this community of abuse and selfishness knows about is the practice of *imagining a neighborly transformation.* Deuteronomy emerges as a primary document for exiles, eventually being pivotal for the formation of Judaism. Dislocation carries with it a temptation to be preoccupied with self, to look out only for number one, to flee the hard places of community formation for the sake of private well-being. One can see that among us; public responsibility is on the wane while even the most privileged desperately work to improve their private estate.

Against such an inclination, the tradition of Deuteronomy relentlessly thinks of society as a *neighborhood* and enjoins attitudes and conduct and policies that enhance neighborliness. Dislocation feeds a self-preoccupying individualism, as evidenced in greed that is now termed "opportunity," in the demise of public health care because it is too costly, and in all the signs that maintenance of public institutions is too expensive, as though taxa-tion were a penalty rather than a necessary neighborly act.

Against that inclination, Deuteronomy insists that life in the economy must be organized for the benefit and well-being of *widows, orphans, and undocumented workers,* that is, immigrants.

This response to dislocation is to insist that the maintenance of a public economy of compassion and justice is a way beyond despair. Thus

> You shall not deprive a resident alien or an orphan of justice; you shall not take a widow's garment in pledge. Remember that you were a slave in Egypt. . . .
>
> When you reap your harvest in your field and forget a sheaf in the field, you shall not go back and get it; it shall be left for the alien, orphan, and, widow, so that the LORD your God may bless you. (Deut. 24:17-19)

A society that cannot be generous in public ways will not be blessed, but will be consumed in its chosen amnesia. And this:

> Every seventh year you shall grant a remission of debts. . . . Do not be hard-hearted or tight-fisted toward your needy neighbor. You shall rather open your hand, willingly lending enough to meet the need, whatever it may be. (Deut. 15:1, 7-8)

This is perhaps the most astonishing command in the Bible. It was the practice in that ancient world, as now, that if one owed money to another, it had to be worked off in regular work payments. The more owed, the more work required. And if one owed enough, one might eventually belong "to the company store." Except that this visionary community set a limit to such debt-related work, in order to preclude the formation of a permanent underclass. And therefore, no matter how great the debt, it was to be worked off for six years and not longer. The residue of debt is canceled. It is clear that Deuteronomy understood that economic practice is a subset of neighborliness and that economic provision must be adjusted in whatever ways necessary to sustain viable community.

Dislocation is a good time to undertake the formation of a permanent underclass. When all are nervous and anxious, there is a temptation to gouge the neighbor, especially the economically vulnerable neighbor. This core tradition of the Bible, however, sees dislocation as a time in which to regroup and reorder public policy for the sake of all of the members of society, motivated by a memory of earlier times of one's own disadvantage that continues to propel us with commanding authority. That is, the laws of public life might be very different if all could remember their own times of vulnerability. Deuteronomy knows that dislocation is a time in which amnesia is a powerful temptation. It is, however, a temptation that must be powerfully and intentionally resisted.

VI

The fourth practice of speech in this community of abandonment and despair, the last I shall mention, concerns *the news of God,* which *creates new social possibility* beyond the shrunken horizons of defeat and submissive docility.

The exiles in Babylon faced an empire that seemed to circumscribe and limit and dictate everything, not unlike the ways in which the all-pervasive *military consumerism* among us seems to circumscribe all of life. The exilic community of ancient Israel came within a whisker of being able to imagine its future only in the terms permitted and sanctioned by Babylon, a sure program for despair and diminishment. Into this scene of shriveling comes the prophet of Isaiah 40–55, the one who funded Handel's *Messiah.* He is the most vigorous, most daring, most imaginative of all the voices of faith in the exile, offering in the midst of the suffering and despair of his people a voice for radical new possibility. This is the remarkable evangelical voice who dares to say defiantly, in the face of imperial power, "Your God reigns" (not theirs) (Isa. 52:7). The God who is here proclaimed anew is the one who announces comfort to exilic Jerusalem beyond comfort, who asserts that the time of dislocation and suffering is over (40:1-2). This is the poet who invites his exilic community to leave exile:

> Depart, depart . . .
> go out from the midst of it. (52:11)

> You shall go out in joy,
>   and be led back in peace. (55:12)

The departure from exile may indeed be geographical, as we have commonly assumed. But likely not. If it is only geographical, then the invitation hardly pertains to us, because we are not going anywhere. My own judgment, however, is that first, the departure is *emotional, liturgical, imaginative*, the process of having a vision of the future of the world (and our future) that is not limited to the fearful dreams of entrenched power, an imagination that is weaned away from the powers that have kept us too long, perhaps the close reckoning of orthodoxy too settled, perhaps excessive self-protection and self-assurance, perhaps the fraudulent comforts of imperial finance and weaponry that serve as narcotics. One can almost sense in this daring poetry of Isaiah the dancing lightness of a small child who refuses the weary soberness of jaded adults who have held the world too long in one position. This poetry invites the exiles to host a large "Otherwise" that amounts to an emotional act of civil disobedience.

Thus Frederick Buechner in his book, *Longing for Home,* can write:

> We carry inside us a *vision of wholeness* that we sense is our true home that beckons us.[1]

> *Joy is home*, and I believe that the tears that come are tears of homesickness.[2]

And then this:

> Woe to us if we forget the homeless ones who have no vote, no power, nobody to lobby for them, who might as well have no faces. . . . Woe to us if we forget our own homelessness. To be homeless the way people like you and me are apt to be homeless is to have homes all over the place but not really to be home in any of them. To be really at home is to be really at peace, and our lives are so intrinsically interwoven that there can be no peace for any of us until there is real peace for all of us.[3]

What Buechner knows so eloquently Isaiah in exile already knows well in the sixth century. And so he says, "You shall go out in joy, you shall come home in peace . . ." (Isa. 55:12) out from under the lying denial and the killing despair of dominant values. Most refused the offer. Most stayed with the empire, which seemed to have all the goodies. Some few took a chance on the poetry. They are the ones who have kept faith for us and who have kept open a future for us, offered in the resounding poetry that persists against the empire and has not been fully silenced, even until now.

VII

Some conclusions:

We are, in church and in society, in big trouble. There are not many places for help or many resources for the trouble we are in. I propose that if the synagogue and the church were serious about the dangerous gospel claims entrusted to them, in this old exilic text the church and the synagogue would offer life anew to our society.

1. This is a tradition, a stream of imagination, *focused upon Yahweh,* a God who causes exiles and who ends them. This Yahweh is a decisive reference point who is not so easily dismissed from public life, as our modern autonomy had imagined. This Yahweh still keeps turning up with awesome authority wherever folk will linger over these texts.

2. This is a tradition enormously *generative,* driven by the news of God not defeated by dislocation but emancipating for a fresh embrace of God's newness. There is no doubt that we are weary with our technological reductionism and jaded by our bureaucratic success. And now this text, in its relentless energy, propels folk into newness where we had not thought previously to go.

3. This tradition is immensely *pluralistic,* not needing to enforce conformity, but instead letting a million voices sound, permitting a million futures to dance before our eyes. It occurs to me that people in charge cannot tolerate pluralism. And so the church, in its cultural dominance, has been a determined vehicle for conformity and coercion. But the church is no longer dominant. This may be a time to replicate our exilic mothers and fathers, who believed that the way into a healed future was to let many voices and many visions play without needing to force all into one.

4. This daring, exuberant exilic offer of possibility is *rooted in deep joy and quiet confidence*—not happiness, not comfort, not ease, not euphoria, not self-indulgence—deep joy and quiet confidence lodged in confidence about God's newness. The exiles chose against atheism, not because they had counted gods, but because they knew that in their denial and despair they could never be self-starters . . . nor can we!

Thus I propose to you an agenda for the kinds of speech the church may offer in our time of dislocation, speech that dominant society regards as subversive, but speech without which we cannot for long stay human:

1. The offer of *voices of sadness and rage and loss*, alternative to denial that inevitably breeds brutality.
2. The invitation of a *voice of holiness* that hosts God's presence, alternative to trivial commoditization by the practice of disciplines that make communion possible, a refusal to accept the world thin and empty, without God.
3. The sounding of a voice of *imaginative, neighborly transformation*, focused on needy neighbors, that refuses privatism, but that envisions a renewed public, willing to pay what is required for the joy of the resident alien.
4. The cadences of *new social possibility*, rooted in the truth of God's good news, refusing to accept the verdict of "impossibility" the world of imperial reason regularly and eagerly champions.

In the deep dislocation where God has now placed us, we must do some new deciding. While the deciding we face is complex and demanding, in the end it comes down to a few large choices . . . a choice of fearful self-preoccupation that invites a shriveled human spirit or a fresh embrace of this buoyant alternative that subverts fearful preoccupation and calls to a large reentry into the pain of the world (denial) and into the possibility of God's newness (despair).

The church and the synagogue have long known some oddities that are germane to a world far from home, a world increasingly reduced to silence, alienated from our mother tongue. Put in Christian parlance, the summons to dislocated folk sounds something like this:

> Softly and tenderly Jesus is calling . . .
> "Come home, come home,
> ye who are weary come home . . . "[4]

6

The Liturgy of Abundance, the Myth of Scarcity

THE MAJORITY OF THE WORLD'S RESOURCES POUR INTO THE UNITED States. And as we Americans grow wealthier and wealthier, money is becoming a kind of narcotic for us. We hardly notice our own prosperity or the poverty of so many others. The great contradiction is that we have more and more money and less and less generosity—less and less public money for the needy, less charity for the neighbor.

Robert Wuthnow, sociologist of religion at Princeton University, has studied stewardship in the church and discovered that preachers do a good job of promoting stewardship. They study it, think about it, explain it well. But folks do not get it. Though many of us are well intentioned, we have invested our lives in consumerism. We have a love affair with "more"—and we will never have enough. Consumerism is not simply a marketing strategy. It has become a demonic spiritual force among us, and the theological question facing us is whether the gospel has the power to help us withstand it.

The Bible starts out with a liturgy of abundance. Genesis 1 is a song of praise for God's generosity. It tells how well the world is ordered. It keeps saying, "It is good, it is good, it is good, it is very good." It declares that God blesses—that is, endows with vitality—the plants and the animals and the fish and the birds and humankind. And it pictures the creator as saying, "Be fruitful and multiply." In an orgy of fruitfulness, everything in its kind is to multiply the overflowing goodness that pours from God's creator spirit. And as you know, the creation ends in Sabbath. God is so overrun with fruitfulness that God says, "I've got to take a break from all this. I've got to get out of the office."

And Israel celebrates God's abundance. Psalm 104, the longest creation poem, is a commentary on Genesis 1. The psalmist surveys creation and names it all: the heavens and the earth, the waters and springs and streams and trees and birds and goats and wine and oil and bread and people and lions. This goes on for twenty-three verses and ends in the twenty-fourth with the psalmist's expression of awe and praise for God and God's creation. Verses 27 and 28 are something like a table prayer. They proclaim, "You give them all food in due season; you feed everybody." The psalm ends by picturing God as a great respirator. It says, "If you give your breath the world will live; if you ever stop breathing, the world will die." But the psalm makes clear that we do not need to worry. God is utterly, utterly reliable. The fruitfulness of the world is guaranteed.

Psalm 150, the last psalm in the book, is an exuberant expression of amazement at God's goodness. It says simply, "Praise Yahweh, praise Yahweh with lute, praise Yahweh with trumpet, praise, praise, praise." Together, these three Scriptures proclaim that God's force of life is loose in the world. Genesis 1 affirms generosity and denies scarcity. Psalm 104 celebrates the buoyancy of creation and rejects anxiety. Psalm 150 enacts abandoning oneself to God and letting go of the need to have anything under control.

Later in Genesis God blesses Abraham, Sarah, and their family. God tells them to be a blessing, to bless the people of all nations. Blessing is the force of well-being active in the world, and faith is the awareness that creation is the gift that keeps on giving. That awareness dominates Genesis until its forty-seventh chapter. In that chapter Pharaoh dreams that there will be a famine in the land, so he gets organized to administer, control, and monopolize the food supply. Pharaoh introduces the principle of scarcity into the world economy. For the first time in the Bible, someone says, "There's not enough. Let's get everything."

Martin Niemöller, the German pastor who heroically opposed Adolf Hitler, was a young man when, as part of a delegation of leaders of the Evangelical Lutheran Church, he met with Hitler in 1933. Niemöller stood at the back of the room and looked and listened. He did not say anything. When he went home, his wife asked him what he had learned that day. Niemöller replied, "I discovered that Herr Hitler is a terribly frightened man."

Because Pharaoh, like Hitler after him, is afraid that there are not enough good things to go around, he must try to have them all. Because he is fearful, he is ruthless. Pharaoh hires Joseph to manage the monopoly. When the crops fail and the peasants run out of food, they come to Joseph. And on behalf of Pharaoh, Joseph says, "What's your collateral?" They give up their land for food, and then, the next year, they give up their cattle. By the third year of the famine they have no collateral but themselves. And that is how the children of Israel become slaves—through an economic transaction.

By the end of Genesis 47 Pharaoh has all the land except that belonging to the priests, which he never touches because he needs somebody to bless him. The notion of scarcity has been introduced into biblical faith. Exodus records the contest between the liturgy of generosity and the myth of scarcity—a contest that still tears us apart today.

The promises of the creation story continue to operate in the lives of the children of Israel. Even in captivity, the people multiply. By the end of Exodus 1 Pharaoh decides that they have become so numerous that he doesn't want any more Hebrew babies to be born. He tells the two midwives Shiphrah and Puah (though we don't know Pharaoh's name, we know theirs) to kill all the newborn boys. But they do not, and the Hebrew babies just keep popping out.

By the end of Exodus, Pharaoh has been as mean, brutal, and ugly as he knows how to be—and as the myth of scarcity tends to be. Finally, he becomes so exasperated by his inability to control the people of Israel that he calls Moses and Aaron to come to him. Pharaoh tells them, "Take your people and leave. Take your flocks and herds and just get out of here!" And then the great king of Egypt, who presides over a monopoly of the region's resources, asks Moses and Aaron to bless him. The powers of scarcity admit to this little community of abundance, "It is clear that you are the wave of the future. So before you leave, lay your powerful hands upon us and give us energy." The text shows that the power of the future is not in the hands of those who believe in scarcity and monopolize the world's resources; it is in the hands of those who trust God's abundance.

1

When the children of Israel are in the wilderness, beyond the reach of Egypt, they still look back and think, "Should we really go? All the world's glory is in Egypt and with Pharaoh." But when they finally turn around and look into the wilderness, where there are no monopolies, they see the glory of Yahweh.

In answer to the people's fears and complaints, something extraordinary happens. God's love comes trickling down in the form of bread. They say, "*Manhue?*"—Hebrew for "What is it?"—and the word *manna* is born. They had never before received bread as a free gift that they could not control, predict, plan for, or own. The meaning of this strange narrative is that the gifts of life are indeed given by a generous God. It's a wonder, it's a miracle, it's an embarrassment, it's irrational, but God's abundance transcends the market economy.

Three things happened to this bread in Exodus 16. First, everybody had enough. But because Israel had learned to believe in scarcity in Egypt, the people started to hoard the bread. When they tried to bank it, to invest it, it turned sour and rotted, because you cannot store up God's generosity. Finally, Moses said, "You know what we ought to do? We ought to do what God did in Genesis 1. We ought to have a Sabbath." Sabbath means that there is enough bread, that we do not have to hustle for our lives every day. There is no record that Pharaoh ever took a day off. People who think their lives consist of struggling to get more and more can never slow down because they will not ever have enough.

When the people of Israel cross the Jordan River into the promised land the manna stops coming. Now they can and will have to grow their food. Very soon Israel suffers a terrible defeat in battle, and Joshua conducts an investigation to find out who or what undermined the war effort. He finally traces their defeat to a man called Achan, who stole some of the spoils of battle and withheld them from the community. Possessing land, property, and wealth makes people covetous, the Bible warns.

We who are now the richest nation are today's main coveters. We never feel that we have enough; we have to have more and more, and this insatiable desire destroys us. Whether we are liberal or conservative Christians, we must confess that the central problem of our lives is that we are torn apart by the conflict between our attraction to the good news of God's abundance and the power of our belief in scarcity—a belief that makes us greedy, mean, and unneighborly. We spend our lives trying to sort out that ambiguity.

The conflict between the narratives of abundance and of scarcity is the defining problem confronting us at the turn of the millennium. The gospel story of abundance asserts that we originated in the magnificent, inexplicable love of a God who loved the world into generous being. The baptismal service declares that each of us has been miraculously loved into existence by God. And the story of abundance says that our lives will end in God, and that this well-being cannot be taken from us. In the words of St. Paul, neither life nor death nor angels nor principalities nor things—nothing can separate us from God.

What we know about our beginnings and our endings, then, creates a different kind of present tense for us. We can live according to an ethic whereby we are not driven, controlled, anxious, frantic, or greedy, precisely because we are sufficiently at home and at peace to care about others as we have been cared for.

But if you are like me, while you read the Bible you keep looking over at the screen to see how the market is doing. If you are like me, you read the Bible on a good day, but you watch Nike ads every day. And the Nike story says that our beginnings are in our achievements, and that we must create ourselves. My wife and I have some young friends who have a four-year-old son. Recently the mother told us that she was about to make a crucial decision. She had to get her son into the right kindergarten because if she didn't, then he would not get into the right prep school. And that would mean not being able to get into Davidson College. And if he didn't go to school there, he would not be connected to the bankers in Charlotte and be able to get the kind of job where he would make a lot of money. Our friends' story is a kind of parable of our notion that we must position ourselves because we must achieve and build our own lives.

According to a bumper sticker, "Whoever dies with the most toys wins." There are no gifts to be given because there is no giver. We end up only with whatever we manage to get for ourselves. This story ends in despair. It gives us a present tense of anxiety, fear, greed, and brutality. It produces child and wife abuse, indifference to the poor, the buildup of armaments, divisions between people, and environmental racism. It tells us not to care about anyone but ourselves—and it is the prevailing creed of American society.

Wouldn't it be wonderful if liberal and conservative church people, who love to quarrel with each other, came to a common realization that the real issue confronting us is whether the news of God's abundance can be trusted in the fact of the story of scarcity? What we know in the secret recesses of our hearts is that the story of scarcity is a tale of death. And the people of God counter this tale by witnessing to the manna. There is a more excellent bread than crass materialism. It is the bread of life, and you do not have to bake it. As we walk into the new millennium, we must decide where our trust is to be placed.

The great question now facing the church is whether our faith allows us to live in a new way. If we choose the story of death, we will lose the land— to excessive chemical fertilizer, or by pumping out the water table for irrigation, perhaps. Or maybe we will only lose it at night, as going out after dark becomes more and more dangerous.

Joshua 24 puts the choice before us. Joshua begins by reciting the story of God's generosity, and he concludes by saying, "I don't know about you, but I and my house will choose the Lord." This is not a church-growth text. Joshua warns the people that this choice will bring them a bunch of trouble. If they want to be in on the story of abundance, they must put away their foreign gods—I would identify them as the gods of scarcity.

Jesus said it more succinctly. You cannot serve God and Mammon. You cannot serve God and do what you please with your money or your sex or your land. And then he says, "Don't be anxious, because everything you need will be given to you." But you must decide. Christians have a long history of trying to squeeze Jesus out of public life and reduce him to a private little savior. But to do this is to ignore what the Bible really says. Jesus talks a great deal about the kingdom of God—and what he means by that is a public life reorganized toward neighborliness.

As a little child, Jesus must often have heard his mother, Mary, singing. And as we know, she sang a revolutionary song, the Magnificat—the anthem of Luke's gospel. She sang about neighborliness; about how God brings down the mighty from their thrones and lifts up the lowly; about how God fills the hungry with good things and sends the rich away empty. Mary did not make up this dangerous song. She took it from another mother, Hannah, who sang it much earlier to little Samuel, who became one of ancient Israel's great revolutionaries. Hannah, Mary, and their little boys imagined a great social transformation. Jesus enacted his mother's song well. Everywhere he went he broke the vicious cycles of poverty, bondage, fear, and death; he healed, transformed, empowered, and brought new life. Jesus' example gives us the mandate to transform our public life.

Telling parables was one of Jesus' revolutionary activities, for parables are subversive reimaginings of reality. The ideology devoted to encouraging consumption wants to shrivel our imaginations so that we cannot conceive of living in any way that would be less profitable for the dominant corporate structures. But Jesus tells us that we can change the world.

The Christian community performs a vital service by keeping the parables alive. These stories haunt us and push us in directions we never thought we would go.

11

Performing what the Bible calls "wonders and signs" was another way in which Jesus enacted his mother's song. These signs—or miracles—may seem odd to us, but in fact they are the typical gifts we receive when the world gets reorganized and placed under the sovereignty of God. Everywhere Jesus goes the world is rearranged: the blind receive their sight, the lame walk, the lepers are cleansed, the deaf hear, the dead are raised, and the poor are freed from debt. The forgiveness of debts is listed last because it is the hardest thing to do—harder even than raising the dead to life. Jesus left ordinary people dazzled, amazed, and grateful; he left powerful people angry and upset, because every time he performed a wonder, they lost a little of their clout. The wonders of the new age of the coming of God's kingdom may scandalize and upset us. They dazzle us, but they also make us nervous. The people of God need pastoral help in processing this ambivalent sense of both deeply yearning for God's new creation and deeply fearing it.

The feeding of the multitudes, recorded in Mark's gospel, is an example of the new world coming into being through God. When the disciples, charged with feeding the hungry crowd, found a child with five loaves and two fishes, Jesus took, blessed, broke, and gave the bread. These are the four decisive verbs of our sacramental existence. Jesus conducted a eucharist, a gratitude. He demonstrated that the world is filled with abundance and freighted with generosity. If bread is broken and shared, there is enough for all. Jesus is engaged in the sacramental, subversive reordering of public reality.

The profane is the opposite of the sacramental. *Profane* means flat, empty, one-dimensional, exhausted. The market ideology wants us to believe that the world is profane—life consists of buying and selling, weighing, measuring, and trading, and then finally sinking into death and nothingness. But Jesus presents an entirely different kind of economy, one infused with the mystery of abundance and a cruciform kind of generosity. Five thousand are fed and twelve baskets of food are left over—one for every tribe of Israel. Jesus transforms the economy by blessing it and breaking it beyond self-interest. From broken Friday bread comes Sunday abundance. In this and in the following account of a miraculous feeding in Mark, people do not grasp, hoard, resent, or act selfishly; they watch as the juices of heaven multiply the bread of earth. Jesus reaffirms Genesis 1.

When people forget that Jesus is the bread of the world, they start eating junk food—the food of the Pharisees and of Herod, the bread of moralism and of power. Too often the church forgets the true bread and is tempted by the junk food. Our faith is not just about spiritual matters; it is about the transformation of the world. The closer we stay to Jesus, the more we will bring a new economy of abundance to the world. The disciples often do not get what Jesus is about because they keep trying to fit him into old patterns—and to do so is to make him innocuous, irrelevant, and boring. But Paul gets it.

In 2 Corinthians 8, Paul directs a stewardship campaign for the early church and presents Jesus as the new economist. Though Jesus was rich, Paul says, "yet for your sakes he became poor, that by his poverty you might become rich." We say it takes money to make money; Paul says it takes poverty to produce abundance. Jesus gave himself to enrich others, and we should do the same. Our abundance and the poverty of others need to be brought into a new balance. Paul ends his stewardship letter by quoting Exodus 16: "And the one who had much did not have too much, and the one who had little did not have too little." The citation is from the story of the manna that transformed the wilderness into abundance.

It is, of course, easier to talk about these things than to live them. Many people both inside and outside of the church haven't a clue that Jesus is talking about the economy. We have not taught them that he is. But we must begin to do so now, no matter how economically compromised we may feel. Our world absolutely requires this news. It has nothing to do with being Republicans or Democrats, liberals or conservatives, socialists or capitalists. It is much more elemental: the creation is infused with the creator's generosity, and we can find practices, procedures, and institutions that allow that generosity to work. Like the rich young man in Mark 10, we all have many possessions. Sharing our abundance may, as Jesus says, be impossible for mortals, but nothing is impossible for God. None of us knows what risks God's spirit may empower us to take. At the turn of the millennium, our faith, ministry, and hope are that the creator will empower us to trust his generosity so that bread may abound.

7   Texts That Linger, Not Yet Overcome

It is clear that God, as rendered in the Bible, is a continually unsettled character, and consequently an unending problem for theology, as theology has been conventionally done in the Christian West. The profound tension between the textual rendering of God and conventional theological settlements constitutes an ongoing interpretive problem for anyone who moves between text and a Christian interpretive community.[1] No one has written more passionately or effectively on this issue than has James Crenshaw, and I have come to believe that his careful, critical work has an intentional thrust against reductionist theological conventions.[2] The problematic character of God in the text may be treated variously under the topics of wrath, anger, capriciousness, hiddenness, etc.[3] Here I shall seek to advance the direction of Crenshaw's acute interest in the issue, in one small way by addressing the question of God's abandoning absence.[4]

1

We may begin our discussion by focusing on four texts, all of which ponder the absence of God by the strong use of the verb *'azav*.

1. Perhaps the obvious place to begin is Psalm 22:1:

> My God, my God, why have you forsaken me?
> Why are you so far from helping me, from the words of
>   my groaning?

This characteristic complaint voices an accusation against God, suggesting that God's (seeming?) absence is unreasonable, unexpected, and inexcusable, and, in fact, reflects God's untrustworthiness. As is well known, this Psalm, with a series of "motivations," expresses a series of petitions that urge Yahweh's presence and active intervention (vv. 11, 19-21a), and culminates in a celebration of rescue.[5] That is, by the end of the poem this abandoning absence of God is overcome, and God is decisively present. We cannot, however, permit the resolution at the end of the poem to nullify the experience and expression of absence at the beginning.[6] Moreover, no hint of fault, blame, or sin on the part of the speaker is expressed, as though the speaker's conduct justified the absence of God. It is clear that God is culpable in the intention of the speaker.

The accusation of v. 1, because it is a complaint, is of course in the mouth of the human (Israelite) speaker. Thus it is possible to say that the human voice has it wrong, that God is not absent but "seems" to be absent (on this, see below). For Christians this accusation against God takes on additional gravity when it occurs on the lips of Jesus (Matt. 27:46, Mark 15:34). It is a common theological strategy among Christians to explain away the abrasion of the opening lines of the psalm, by observing that the line quoted in the Gospel narratives only introduces the whole implied psalm, again as though the implied ending nullifies the expressed beginning. In an important exception to this conventional Christian strategy, Jürgen Moltmann takes the gospel reiteration of Psalm 22:1 with theological seriousness.[7] God is absent and is said to be absent. The narrative of the crucifixion of Jesus is a Christian articulation of that absence of God that causes the world to revert to chaos.[8]

2. The capacity to explain Psalm 22:1 away, because it is a human articulation of absence that may be a misperception of God, is an equally possible strategy in Lamentations 5:20:

> Why have you forgotten us completely?
> Why have you forsaken ('azav) us these many days?

Whereas Psalm 22 deals with an unspecified situation, Lam. 5:20 is context specific. The verse pertains to the collapse of the symbolic (as well as political) world of Jerusalem (and of Judaism) over which Israel grieved massively.[9] The physical loss experienced by Jews in the crisis of 587 B.C.E. is matched by the powerful sense of intimate, personal, religious loss. The destruction of Jerusalem signifies God's absence and happens as a consequence of God's (unwarranted?) absence.[10] The interrogative form of v. 20 is the same as in Psalm 22:1 with *lamah*. The speaker does not question that God has abandoned. The abandonment by Yahweh is taken as a given. In asking "why," the speaker does not seek an explanation from God, but seeks to assert that the absence of God is inexplicable and inexcusable.

Verse 20 is framed in the last strophe of vv. 19-22 by three striking assertions, each of which functions in relation to the desperate accusation of v. 20. In v. 19, the speaker utters a wondrous doxology, appealing to the enthronement liturgies, acknowledging God's sovereign power. The effect of this verse is to make the absence of v. 20 all the more scandalous, for the one who "reigns forever" can hardly be absent. Verse 21 looks behind v. 20 to v. 19, and on the basis of the doxology issues an urgent imperative for God's action, thus characteristically following complaint with petition.[11] In spite of the doxology and petition, however, the final verse (v. 22) returns to and reasserts the conclusion of v. 20:

> But instead you have completely rejected us;
> you have been very angry with us.[12]

And thus the poem ends. The accusatory verbs of v. 20 ("forget, abandon") are reinforced by "reject, be angry" (v. 22). Unlike Psalm 22:1, there is no resolution in this dread-filled complaint. The poem ends abruptly and without any response from God. The effect is to confirm God's absence, a fickle absence, and leaves the words "forget, abandon" ringing in Israel's exilic ears.

3. The enduring echo of "forget, abandon" in the exilic literature apparently takes on liturgic form as evidenced in Is. 49:14. That verse is introduced by the rubric, "But Zion said . . ." This is presumably a stylized, often reiterated liturgic complaint. Indeed, this usage is plausibly a reference back to and quotation of Lam. 5:20, given the propensity of exilic Isaiah to be a response to Lamentations.[13] To be sure, the two defining terms, 'azav and šakaḥ, are here in reverse order, but the intention is the same. The complaint, which we have seen already in Lam. 5:20 as well as in Psalm 22:1, is that Yahweh is unfaithful and neglectful. Moreover, it is Yahweh's failure to be faithfully present in Israel that results in the suffering and shame of the exile.

The statement of v. 14, however, is lodged in the midst of a proclamation of salvation, whereby the assurance of Yahweh intends to dispute and overcome the accusatory claim of Israel. Thus, in v. 13 Yahweh is assigned two recurring words of assurance, "comfort" (nhm) and "compassion" (rhm). In direct response to the complaint of v. 14, Yahweh now speaks in the first person, using the term "compassion" and three times "forget" by way of denying the accusation of v. 13. It is worth noting, though perhaps not important, that Yahweh's response does not use a word to negate the accusation of 'azav. The accent is placed on "forget" in the denial of Yahweh.

Given the assurance of Yahweh in the third person (v. 13) and in the first person (v. 15), it is not completely clear how the assurances are related to the complaint. It is easiest to take the assurance as a refutation and denial of the complaint. That is, Israel seemed to be forgotten and forsaken, but was not. On that reading, the complaint of Lam. 5:20 was mistaken. A possible alternative is that Israel is momentarily forgotten by Yahweh, but finally, in the end, Yahweh does not forget. Such a reading points us to our fourth and final text.

4. Thus far, all three texts (Psalm 22:1, Lam. 5:20, Isa. 49:14) have been on the lips of Israel. This fact still allows for the claim that Yahweh "seemed" to Israel to abandon, that Israel "experienced" abandonment, but in fact Israel had it wrong and was not abandoned by Yahweh. Such a reading is of course possible, but it goes well beyond the plain sense of the text, which offers no qualification or ambiguity about the accusation.

In our fourth text, Isa. 54:7-8, that possible "protection" of Yahweh from the accusation of Israel is excluded, for now the word 'azav is on the lips of Yahweh.[14] The poetry uses the image of barren wife, abandoned wife, and widow.[15] Already in v. 6 the term 'azav is used in parallel to "cast off" (ma'as), both terms as passive participles, affirming that Yahweh has taken the disruptive actions.

In vv. 7-8, Yahweh continues to speak in the first person:

> For a brief moment I abandoned you (*'azavtika*) . . .
> In overflowing wrath, for a moment
>   I hid my face (*histortik*) from you.

The two words ("abandoned, hid") are straightforward and unambiguous. Yahweh did abandon! Yahweh has abandoned Israel and readily admits it. In these verses, moreover, no blame is assigned to Israel as cause of the abandonment, though Yahweh says, "In overflowing wrath." From the text itself, such "wrath" could as well be capriciousness on the part of Yahweh as righteous, warranted indignation.

To be sure, these two admissions whereby Yahweh concedes that Israel has been abandoned are promptly countered by two assurances:

> . . . with great compassion (*rahamim*) I will gather you . . .
> . . . with everlasting love (*hesed olam*) I will have compassion
>   on you (*rahamtika*).

It is profoundly important that the two positives do not nullify the two negatives, as the positive may nullify the negative in 49:14-15. Here the statements refer to a sequence of actions and experiences, whereby compassion comes after an acknowledged abandonment. This is reinforced by the word "again" (*'odh*) in v. 9, which admits one abandonment but assures that there will not be a second one. This use of *'odh* is closely paralleled to its use in Gen. 8:21, 9:11, which admits that there has indeed been one angry flood, but there will not be another (cf. Isa. 54:10).

This fourth text, Isa. 54:7-8, belongs in the same theological horizon as Ps. 22:1, Lam. 5:20, and Isa. 49:14, all of which are preoccupied with Israel's experience of bereftment caused by Yahweh's unwarranted inattentiveness. This fourth text, however, is of another sort, because it is in Yahweh's own mouth, and because Yahweh concedes that compassion and everlasting love come *after* the abandonment.

Now all of this is commonplace and well established in Crenshaw's work. Of course other texts could be cited and other companion themes of "darkness" could be considered. God's face is indeed darkened in silence, absence, anger, and fickleness. My intent is not to establish an exegetical point that is already amply recognized by readers of Israel's text. It is rather to inquire about what to do with such texts in reading communities that want to override such texts with sweeping assurances about Yahweh's presence, fidelity, and graciousness. Thus my study is an exercise in adjudicating the tension between large theological claims and the awkward specificity of texts.

II

There is no doubt that these assertions about Yahweh's abandoning activity are problematic for any theology that wants finally to assert the unambiguous fidelity of God. A variety of interpretive strategies are available and much practiced whereby these troublesome texts can be overcome, but in each case the alternative strategy does not appear to take the direct statement of the text with full seriousness. They may be regarded as adequate resolutions of the problem, unless one is intensely committed to facing the concreteness of the text, a commitment we may take to be important for any responsible reading of the text.

We may identify five such strategies that are frequently employed:

1. It is easiest and most common simply to *disregard such "texts of darkness."* It is for the most part impossible to make use of all texts in any interpretive reading, or all texts at once, and surely impossible to attend to all of them if one wants to present a "seamless" reading, for the text itself is disjointed and disruptive, and filled with contradictions, ambiguities, and incongruities. They render the text as a whole as "unreadable" in our usual theological readings.[16]

On the basis of that "unreadable" textual reality, reading communities of every kind, including church communities (but also academic communities) tend to be selective. Indeed, it is my judgment that serious readers tend to be "selective fundamentalists," whether liberal or conservative theological readers, or critical readers. That is, readers pick out texts on the basis of hidden or explicit criteria, take those texts with great attentiveness or even urgency, and let the other texts drop out of the working repertoire. An easy example, of course, is the church's lectionary, which operates around such principles that even some verses in the chosen texts are habitually silenced. Part of recent hermeneutical activity is the insistence that those silenced, dismissed texts must be sounded again.

2. The "darkened" character of Yahweh is justified by *the sin of Israel,* thus suggesting that God's silence, absence, wrath, or infidelity is warranted in light of Israel's sin and disobedience.[17] Such an interpretive posture posits a tight moral structure, so that Yahweh responds with precision to moral affront.[18] There are of course many texts that support such a view.

There are other texts, however, including those we have cited, that do not claim such an exact calculus, or even suggest Israel's culpability. Moreover, there are texts (as Job) that voice a "darkened" response of Yahweh that is disproportionate to any available affront. There are sufficient texts to warrant the judgment that there is a wild dimension to Yahweh's "darkness" that runs well beyond any tight moral equation. Israel's experience of Yahweh's "darkness" runs well beyond moral justification when the texts are taken seriously.

3. There is a great propensity to explain away the "darkened" aspect of Yahweh (in our case abandonment) by claiming that the accusation made against Yahweh and the desperate plea for presence addressed to God are a case of *human misperception and mistakenness*. That is, God "seems" to be abandoning, but in truth is not. Such a human "experience" is asserted by Israel in good faith, and there may be a "subjective" dimension of reality to this claim, but it is theologically not true. It is only in the eyes of the beholder.

This is of course not as difficult to claim in our first three cases (Ps. 22:1, Lam. 5:20, Isa. 49:14), because the statements are all on the lips of Israel, and no data is offered beyond the "sense" of the speaker. Thus resort is often taken to the stratagem that claims that this is only "human speech," which is not finally reliable. The case is more difficult in Isa. 54:7-8 where the utterance is Yahweh's own, that is, an oracle that purports to be God's utterance. Even here, of course, critical awareness can readily claim that even this speech is "human speech," done by a human author, in this case "Second Isaiah," so that even this more insistent affirmation is explained away as not theologically reliable.[19]

This common interpretive procedure, however, is deeply problematic. It appeals to theological-dogmatic convictions nowhere grounded in the particular texts, but imposed upon the text in order to dismiss a reading that on the face of it is not in doubt. Moreover, if one explains away as "human and mistaken" such self-assertions made by Yahweh, one is hard put to draw the line and treat with seriousness the textual self-disclosures of Yahweh that one prefers. It may be claimed that the dismissal of the assertion is "canonical," that is, read in relation to many other texts that say otherwise and are judged to be more central.[20] Such a claim, however, is characteristically reductionist, and flattens the dialectic that, in my judgment, belongs properly to canonical reading.[21]

4. A more subtle approach to this same "subjective" verdict voiced in the text is the logical, philosophical claim that even though Yahweh is genuinely "experienced" as one who abandons, the experience of God's abandoning contains within it an assumption of cosmic, primordial presence, thus giving us a *dialectical notion of "presence in absence" or "absence in presence."*[22] That is, even speculation about God's abandoning absence (which never posits God's non-existence) affirms God's "background" presence even in experienced absence. This is, I take it, a quite sophisticated form of a "subjective-objective" distinction, which seeks to honor fully the *lived experience* of Israel, while at the same time guarding against an *ontological* dismissal of God which Israel would not countenance. This strategy is based upon the theological affirmation that there would be no world without God, no world in which to issue complaint and accusation against God, for the world is "held into existence" by God.

This is a powerful and logically coherent position, and I have no desire to combat it. I suggest only that a) that it is a way of reasoning that is subtle in ways that Israel would not entertain, and b) it requires a judgment that is against the clear, uncomplicated, and unreserved statement of the text. As a result, even after this argument, we are still left with our guiding question, what shall one do with texts such as these?

5. Finally, a popular stratagem is an appeal to the "evolution" of "the religion of Israel" that includes the *"evolution" of Yahweh*, the subject of that religion. That hypothesis proposes that Israel's religion and Israel's God "developed" from primitivism to the nobility of "ethical monotheism," culminating, perhaps, in Second Isaiah. Thus, there may have been a time when Yahwism (and Yahweh) were understood in quite primitive terms. There may have been a time when Yahweh was excessively "dark" in terms of capriciousness, infidelity, violence, absence, and silence. But Yahweh has "evolved" toward fidelity, peaceable generosity, justice, and forgiveness.

That hypothesis of course has been duly critiqued as a reflection of Hegelianism or a reflection of a nineteenth-century milieu dominated by something like Darwinism.[23] Nonetheless, there is, of course, something substantive to the hypothesis, as there regularly is in any hypothesis that captures scholarly imagination over a long period of time. It is the case that there are important changes in the character of Yahweh. Moreover, given a certain literary analysis, one can insist upon a directional inclination to that change. It is the most standard critique of the hypothesis that the change is said to be progressive and unilaterally developmental. In addition to that claim, the critique that is most important for our purposes is the correlative of progressive developmentalism, that as each *novum* appears in the character of Yahweh, the previous portrayals of the character of Yahweh may be sloughed off as now irrelevant and "superseded."

I shall want to insist in what follows that textually, there is no supersessionism, but that what has transpired in the life of Yahweh endures as text, and therefore as data for theological understanding. This remembered character of Yahweh continues to exercise important influence over the whole of Israel's articulation of Yahweh. Specifically, because Israel has texts of God's abandoning, which it evidently has, the character of Yahweh never outgrows or supersedes that remembered reality, which continues to be present textually and therefore substantively both for Yahweh and the community of Yahweh. As a consequence, neither Yahweh nor the interpreters of Yahweh may pretend that such behavior has not happened in the ongoing life of Yahweh with Israel, and may not act as though these textual markings do not continue to be present and available to Yahweh in Yahweh's life with Israel.[24]

Thus I suggest that all five strategies—disregard of such texts, justification through sin, judgment that it only "seems so," philosophical subtlety, and evolutionary supersessionism—are unpersuasive approaches to the problem. Each of these attempts arises from a theological impetus that lies outside the horizon of the text itself, and each of them imports a conviction that is contrary to the unmistakable claim of the text itself. All of these inadequate strategies seek to protect the character of Yahweh from the passionate experience and conviction of Israel with Yahweh. Israel is clear that Yahweh need not and cannot be protected; Yahweh must run the risks that belong to Yahweh's way of being present/absent in the memory and life of Israel.

III

I propose now to suggest an alternative interpretive response to these texts of abandonment, and by implication to all texts that testify to Yahweh's "darkened" life.

1. An alternative approach to these "darkened" texts will need to move from a *metaphysical* to a *dramatic* approach to interpretation. A conventional approach to Christian theology that posits a "nature of God" with which to challenge these texts apparently operates with a notion of a God "out there" who exists independent of these texts.[25] Such a view may be plausible from some other perspective, but it is of little help in taking the specificity of the biblical text seriously. Such a posited "nature" outside the text stands as a criterion with which to justify or explain away a text without facing its concrete claim seriously. Indeed, such an approach cannot take such texts with theological seriousness, because matters are settled on grounds other than the text and in other arenas.

A consequence of such an approach is that we are still left with the problem, what to do with the text. An alternative approach that shuns the escape of a metaphysical criterion is to take the texts in a dramatic way, as a script for a drama.[26] The biblical text then becomes "the real thing" in terms of plot and character, and there is no appeal behind the text or elsewhere. From such a perspective, when God asserts, "For a brief moment I have abandoned you," we have a God who abandons Israel for a brief moment. That is what Yahweh says, what Yahweh does, and who Yahweh is.

The move toward a dramatic sense of the text permits the reading community to stay with the terms of the text, even with its contradictions, incongruities, and unwelcome lines. Thus the text is "unreadable," not because of a poor redactional outcome, but because the subject and character who dominates the plot does not conform to our flattened reading propensity, theological or critical. The character who has once uttered these lines and committed these acts remains always the character who has once uttered these lines and committed these acts. There is more to this character than these particular lines, but these lines become inescapably part of who this character is, no matter what other renderings, actions, and utterances may follow. That is, this approach comes to the text prepared to treat the text "realistically" and "literally," if "literal" means not "factual," not canonically reduced, but according to the concrete utterance of the text.[27]

2. But consider what it means to take the text "realistically," I have found enormously helpful the distinction of Richard Lanham between *homo seriosus* and *homo rhetoricus*.[28] Lanham characterizes the model interpreter in this way:

> The serious man possesses a central self, an irreducible identity. These selves combine into single, homogeneously real society which constitutes a referent reality . . . This referent society is in turn contained in a physical nature itself referential, standing "out there," independent of man.[29]

By contrast,

> Rhetorical man is an actor; his reality public, dramatic. His sense of identity, his self, depends on the reassurance of daily histrionic reenactment. He is thus centered in time and concrete local event. The lowest common denominator of his life is a social situation. And his motivations must be characteristically lucid, agonistic . . . He is thus committed to no single construction of the world; much rather, to prevailing in the game at hand.[30]

The important difference is that the "serious man" appeals to an "out there" reference. It is a curious fact that common cause in this category includes those who grasp at metaphysics and the "historical critics" who assess the rhetoric of the text in terms of an outside historical reference. Both metaphysicians and historical critics trim and shave the rhetoric of the text to fit some other criterion. By contrast, those who value rhetoric in a central way recognize that speech constitutes reality in some decisive way. The world of "Rhetorical Man" is

> teeming with roles, situations, strategies, interventions, but . . . no master role, no situation of situations, no strategy for outflanking all strategies . . . no neutral point of rationality from the vantage point of which the 'merely rhetorical' can be identified and held in check.[31]

It is clear that this dispute is as old as Plato and Aristotle with the Sophists. And it is clear that our dominant educational, intellectual tradition is a powerful advocacy toward Plato and Aristotle and a facile dismissal of the Sophists, without attending to the powerful ways in which even Plato and Aristotle are rhetoricians.[32] Thus the critique of Fish goes farther than that of Lanham. It suggests that even the "serious man" in fact makes a claim for reality in terms of the effectiveness of utterance.

What to do with the "dark texts" depends upon where one is in this dispute between rhetoric and "seriousness." If one seriously assumes a reference out there, then these texts must be disregarded, toned down, justified, or explained away, in order to suit that outside reference. If we take rhetoric as constitutive, however, then the reference "inside the drama" must yield to these texts and take them with defining seriousness. Richard Rorty makes the distinction:

> There are two ways of thinking about various things . . . The first . . . thinks of truth as a vertical relationship between representations and what is represented. The second . . . thinks of truth horizontally—as the culminating reinterpretation of our predecessors' reinterpretation of their predecessors' reinterpretation. . . . It is the difference between regarding truth, goodness, and beauty as eternal objects which we try to locate and reveal, and regarding them as artifacts whose fundamental design we often have to alter.[33]

Fish concludes, of Rorty's verdict,

> It is the difference between serious and rhetorical man. It is the difference that remains.[34]

My argument here, which seems to me inescapable if the texts are to be taken seriously and if Crenshaw is correct about the persuasive intentionality of speech, is that rhetoric constitutes the character of Yahweh.[35] And so the Yahweh of the Bible is indeed a "dark-sided" character who does abandon and who acts sometimes in unfaithfulness. Focus on the text rather than on a reference "out there" gives us no character other than this one.

3. But we are not yet agreed on what it means to take the text seriously or how to take the text seriously. I cite two interpreters who well articulate what I regard as two quite distinct alternative approaches.

In his "canonical approach" to the text, Brevard S. Childs is a "serious" reader who does indeed take the text seriously. That is beyond question. In a series of books, Childs has pondered "canonical" reading.[36] In his most recent and most mature book, it is now more clear than in his earlier work, that Childs means by "canonical" reading the text according to Christian doctrinal norms and categories:[37]

> It is one thing to suggest that biblical scholars have not adequately resolved the problem of biblical referentiality; it is quite another to suggest that it is a non-issue. Moreover, I would argue that the attempt of many literary critics to by-pass the problem of biblical reality and refuse to distinguish between text and the reality of its subject matter severely cripples the theological enterprise of Biblical Theology. It is basic to Christian theology to reckon with an extra-biblical reality, namely with the resurrected Christ who evoked the New Testament Witness. When H. Frei, in one of his last essays, spoke of 'midrash' as a text-creating reality, he moved in a direction, in my opinion, which for Christian theology can only end in failure.[38]

In his response to Stanley Hauerwas and James Barr, Childs concludes that "narrative interpretation"

> avoids for a time the difficult problems of referentiality involved in the term history. . . . In a word, the term "story" is not strong enough to support the function assigned to the Bible. Indeed Christians have always believed that we are not saved by a text or by a narrative, but by the life, death, and resurrection of Jesus Christ in time and space.[39]

It becomes clear that Childs' understanding of God in the text, an "extra-biblical reality," is not construed or nuanced according to the detail of the text, but is a reference that is known apart from and at times over against the text. This theological reference must move

> from a description of the biblical witnesses to the object toward which these witnesses point, that is, to their subject matter, substance, or res.[40]

Childs' comments following this statement indicate that he is aware of the dangers in what he suggests, but he proceeds on that basis. Childs is interested in "the reality constitutive of these biblical witnesses."[41] That "reality" is not only "testified to in the Bible." It is

> that living reality known and experienced as the exalted Christ through the Holy Spirit within the present community of faith.[42]

In such a christological formulation as Childs makes central to his perspective, the text as such is subordinated to other claims. A consequence is that the "dark texts" exercise almost no influence upon Childs' interpretation and argument.

A sharp contrast to the approach of Childs occurs in the powerful work of David Blumenthal, who takes his beginning points from the brutality of the holocaust.[43] In contrast to the "canonical reading" of Childs, Blumenthal reads texts "*seriatim* . . . one after another, one by one in succession, which matches the way we live. "We live *seriatim*."[44] This approach yields an accent upon "caesura, fragmentedness, irruption," of course the very matters which Childs wants to exclude.[45]

With relentless determination, Blumenthal insists upon attending to all the texts:

> By contrast, I choose to engage seriously the texts as we have received them. . . . There is, thus, for me, a certain sacredness to the tradition, prima facie, and I try to work within it. For this reason, I reject attempts to "clean up" the Psalms, to interpret away the rage, to make them more "pious."[46]

Blumenthal mentions, as we have also, that historicism and an assumption of moral evolution are two ways to dispose of parts of the text with which one does not agree.[47] Of course he rejects any such a maneuver. By attending *seriatim* to all of the texts, Blumenthal comes to the interpretive conclusion that the God of the Bible "is abusive, but not always."[48] In any case, he makes much room for "dark" texts that Childs drops from purview.

It is important that both Blumenthal and Childs allow for plurivocity in the text. Blumenthal judges,

> In the end, the text has more than one meaning, the reader reads on more than one level, and the teacher teaches more than one meaning. Text and life itself are multifaceted; interpretation is multidimensional. Plurivocity is normal; not hierarchy, not the single authoritative teaching. . . . Plurivocity is, thus, not only normal; it is normative, it is what the norm should be.[49]

Childs agrees, "There is a 'reader response' required by any responsible theological reflection."[50] But Childs, of course, qualifies such an allowance:

> Yet it is crucial to theological reflection that canonical restraints be used and that reader response be critically tested in the light of different witnesses of the whole Bible. . . . There is a biblical rule of faith which sets the standard for family resemblance. . . . Once the task of discerning the kerygmatic content of the witnesses has been pursued, it is fully in order to offer an analogical extension of this kerygmatic message by means of a modern reader response.[51]

This qualification of course causes Childs to part decisively from Blumenthal in the end, concerning "dark" texts.

IV

That still leaves us with the question of what to do with these texts that are there as Blumenthal insists, but texts that are enormously problematic, as Childs insists. My suggestion is that we take a "naïvely realistic" view of the text as a "script" of Yahweh's past. Such naïveté, for this purpose, overrides our critical judgments. Without a hypothesis of moral evolution, it is clear that Yahweh "moves on" as a character in the text, as any character surely will move on in the drama.[52] Thus these texts are in Yahweh's *past*, but they are at the same time assuredly *in* Yahweh's past. I propose, with an analogue from "the enduring power of the past" in therapeutic categories, that these "past texts" are enduringly painful memories still available to the character of Yahweh, mostly not operative, but continuing to work even in the present. They must therefore be taken seriously even in the canonical, "final form" of the text.

This means that a "truer" picture of Yahweh cast in canonical or theological form has moved beyond these texts, but has not superseded these texts, as no human person understood in depth ever supersedes or scuttles or outgrows such ancient and powerful memories. There linger in the character of Yahweh ancient memories (texts) that belong to the "density" of Yahweh and that form a crucial residue of Yahweh's character. Yahweh may not be in a "truer" "canonical" understanding, a God who abandons. But that past marking of Yahweh is still potentially available in the current life of Yahweh (for the text lingers), and must in any case be taken as a crucial part of the career of Yahweh. Yahweh cannot simply will away that past, nor can the interpreters of Yahweh.

For the interpreting community (especially for the religious communities of interpretation, but also for the academic community) that intends to face the fullness of the text, the witness to Yahweh and the interpreters of the witness must take into full account that past and those memories that are in important ways still present, available, and potentially operative. This in turn suggests that it is faithful to the text and healthy for the reading community that there is in this shared, read past a "darkness" that has wounded, troubled, and betrayed those with whom Yahweh has to do. This past of wound, trouble, and betrayal, moreover, still tells in the present. I suggest that such a recovery of the past is not like "critical excavation," for it is not a past that is over and done, but a past that persists like any such held script.[53] Full embrace of such texts permits the interpretive community to embrace fully its theological past, which is marked by abandonment (and the other dimensions of "darkness"). It is not necessary to claim that such a "dark" dimension is normative or presently operative, but only that it has been there in the past and continues to be present in the present. Thus the God of "steadfast love and mercy" is at the same time also the God who has abandoned, and all current steadfastness bears the wounding mark of that ancient, undenied reality.

Such an interpretive strategy affirms that the canonical text is indeed the full telling of the tale of Yahweh, a tale that has odd and unpleasant dimensions to it.

1. As an interpretive perspective, such a procedure permits some thematic closure in the direction that Childs wants to go, but not such closure that it eliminates the candor of the text itself, which has generated the candor of Blumenthal. It occurs to me that while many historical critics insistently resist Childs' closure, such historical critics finally make common cause with Childs, though for very different reasons. Childs tends to shave the text to fit "the creed," whereas historical critics have tended to shave the text to fit Enlightenment reasonableness that wants to eliminate disruption and incongruity in the text. Neither "canonical" nor "critical" readers entertain the naïveté to permit a rendering of the text as the dramatic reality of this God with this people.

2. But my main concern is not interpretive theory. Rather my concern is pastoral responsibility, the kind of pastoral responsibility that belongs to any "classic" read in a theologically serious interpretive community.[54] First, I propose that seeing these texts as a past pertinent to the present, even if now suppressed or denied, permits the interpretive community to see fully who Yahweh has been and potentially is. There is no cover-up of who this God is, no notion that this character can be made to conform to our preferred Enlightenment or orthodox categories of reading. A "second naïveté" permits the reading community to take this God with theological seriousness in all of Yahweh's consternating Jewishness, in all of Yahweh's refusal of domestication.[55]

Second, if this character is understood as a real live agent who concerns the life of the reader or the reading community, the reader is thereby authorized and permitted to entertain "dark" dimensions of one's own life (or one's community) as palpable theological dimensions of reality. Both canonical and critical reading that fend off the "dark" texts encourage denial and cover-up of the intimate savageness of life. But when the reading community can see that brutality, abusiveness, and abandonment are live and present in the past of this God, it is credible to take the same dimension in one's own life as past realities that continue to have potential power in the present.

It is not at all my intention to take a therapeutic or instrumental approach to the character of Yahweh. Nonetheless theological, interpretive, textual candor does have important pastoral consequences. The only way beyond such woundedness is through such woundedness. That ancient woundedness perdures in text and in life. But when voiced and accepted, as the text invites us to do, that ancient woundedness is robbed of its present authority. As long as one pretends that these texts are not "back there," a terrible denial is required, which denies movement into a healing present and a healed future.

It is a delight to honor James Crenshaw who has thought and written most persistently and most honestly about this "dark" side of the text and its God. Crenshaw has indeed shown us that critical analysis and pastoral realism can live close together. Together they can make a pact to engage in denial and cover-up. But they need not. This text, when read without too many protections (canonical or critical), does not protect in such ways. A refusal to deny or censure invites the movement of this Character and the reading community into new dimensions of peaceableness.

8   Crisis-Evoked, Crisis-Resolving Speech

It is clear that Old Testament theology cannot effectively advance by focusing on conventional *conceptual* content in the text.[1] A conceptual focus moves too quickly to systematic, dogmatic categories and thereby misses most of the evocative, transformative power and intention of the text.[2] If we move from conceptual, ideational approaches, however, it is not clear what alternative approach might be most compelling and most responsible. In this presentation, the alternative to a conceptual approach that I wish to test is to consider Israel's *most characteristic speech about God* as the beginning place for Old Testament theology. "Most characteristic speech" might be determined quantitatively, that is, to do a word count to see what speech is most frequent. And that more than likely would not be an unreliable indicator of the center of Israel's expressed faith.

1

An alternative to "most frequent" (which I pursue here) is to focus on the speech to which Israel "regresses" in times of most acute crisis. That is, the most reliable clues about speech may not be frequency of use, but the most relied upon in times of stress. I use the term "regress" in the sense of falling back on what is most habitual and elemental when the occasion is so dangerous and destabilizing as to preclude intentional speech. I think of the ways in which we fall back on the phrasings of childhood or family nurture in times of acute stress, going behind the speech we might like to present when we are more fully in control.

Thus I inquire about the interface between *speech* and *crisis*. I use the word "crisis" to refer to those occasions in Israel's life and faith when its communal existence as a sociopolitical community was at risk, and when Israel's life with Yahweh was placed in jeopardy.[3] That is, such a "crisis" has both an historical-political and a theological dimension; and I imagine that in Israel's self-presentation, the two (historical-political and theological) are never confused but are never fully separated either. Every crisis likely concerns both dimensions of Israel's existence. Such moments of threat are what Paul Ricoeur terms "limit experiences" that require "limit expressions."[4] It is my sense that such "limit-expressions" drive Israel to speech that is most elemental and characteristic, what Israel was required and permitted to say in times of sociotheological danger.

Thus it is my thought that the "crisis" evokes certain modes and forms of speech, that is, brings to out-loud articulation certain expressions that may be long latent in the community, but seem neither possible nor necessary for utterance until the time of concrete risk. As the crisis evokes such speech that we take as Israel's most characteristic speech, the speech turns back to address the crisis that evoked it, and provides a resolution of the crisis, insofar as speech can resolve sociotheological crisis. Thus, I understand such speech to have a dialectical relation to crisis, first wrought through the crisis and then spoken over the crisis in order to permit Israel's life (sociopolitical and theological) to extend in, through, and beyond the crisis.

I propose that in such speech practice in crisis, we are provided clues to Israel's most characteristic speech (whether or not it is the most frequent), and that in this most characteristic speech we arrive at a focus and beginning point for Old Testament theology. Thus we shall be attentive for the *words* that are characteristically uttered, for the *sentences* in which these words are characteristically embedded, and for the *genre* in which the sentences are characteristically situated.[5]

In what follows, I will consider three such crises in Israel's life and faith, and in each case consider a text which on any reading appears to be evoked by the crisis and seeks to resolve the crisis. I will present some provisional conclusions, and finally take up three texts that respond to this "most characteristic speech."

II

The first crisis I will comment upon is the violation of the Sinai covenant in the incident of the golden calf in Exodus 32. According to conventional source criticism, Exodus 32–34 follows in the "early source" immediately after the Sinai events of theophany and covenant in Exodus 24. That is, the materials in chapters 25–31, whether later or not, are in any case of a very different kind, from a different source.[6]

The crisis of covenant-breaking, in this narrative, concerns the sin of Aaron and Israel in the making of the calf (32:30-31), Yahweh's resolve to punish (vv. 33-34), and the plague against Israel instituted by Yahweh (v. 35). It is clear that Israel's life with Yahweh is in jeopardy. (It is of course exceedingly difficult to determine what is "historical" in this narrative. First, the text in some important way is linked to the later narrative account of 1 Kings 12, thus making one extremely cautious about any "historicity" in Exodus 32. Second, the "facticity" of the Sinai tradition is exceedingly problematic, no doubt shaped as it is for ideological purposes.[7] I do not purpose to adjudicate the relationship between "historical" and ideological elements in the text, but to take the text, as it is surely intended, as a paradigmatic account of covenantal crisis.) Even though we recognize the problematic character of the text, for our purposes it is enough to see that this text witnesses to a crisis in which we may attend to Israel's "most characteristic speech."

After the tense negotiations between Yahweh and Moses in chapter 33, wherein Moses seeks assurances from Yahweh for Israel's continued life, we arrive at chapter 34, at the awesome theophany Yahweh has just promised in 33:21-23. This theophany is enormously important for Moses and Israel, for on it hangs the potential for Israel's political future. Moreover, the theophany is as dangerous as it is important, for there is an unresolved fierceness about Yahweh in this confrontation.

The dangerous coming of Yahweh (34:5) eventuates in the utterance of Yahweh (34:6-7). We arrive at the first of our three texts that I take as "most characteristic" of Israel's speech. The text is situated in and evoked by the fracture of the covenant of Sinai. Yahweh would not have spoken in this way if there had not been the violation of covenant. It is not known in this moment of the covenant whether Israel can survive its disastrous affront against Yahweh. And if the possibility of covenant is not known, then it is also not known if Israel has any future in the world. Everything for Israel, everything theological and sociopolitical, depends upon this utterance of Yahweh evoked by the crisis of broken covenant.

So now Yahweh speaks. Israel receives from Yahweh in this awesome moment a divine oracle, an utterance out of God's own mouth (34:6-7). It is Yahweh, in the crisis, who is permitted now to speak as Yahweh has never before spoken in Israel. Or should we better say, Yahweh is now required to speak as Yahweh has never had to speak before. The crisis for Israel is deep and irreversible, and now Israel's text gives an offer of Israel's "most characteristic speech," expressed as divine oracle, as an utterance on God's own lips.

The oracle is in two parts. In the first part, Yahweh presents Yahweh's own self as utterly faithful and generous:

> The LORD, the LORD,
> a God merciful and gracious,
> slow to anger,
> and abounding in steadfast love and faithfulness,
> keeping steadfast love for the thousandth generation,
> forgiving iniquity and transgression and sin . . . (vv. 6-7a)

What is important for us is that this oracle provides most of the working vocabulary whereby Israel will subsequently (as, for example, in the Psalms) speak to God and about God. This rich array of terms . . . merciful, gracious, steadfast love, faithfulness, forgiving . . . bespeaks a God who is generous in fidelity, thus providing a basis for Israel's future, even after the disaster of Exodus 32. It is in this crisis that Israel hears (not speaks!) its most characteristic "God-talk," that it had not heard before. It is, moreover, to the crisis that God's oracle speaks, for the oracle asserts that even the episode of the golden calf has not nullified God's covenantal fidelity for Israel.

Many scholars have noted that this originary speech in God's mouth stands at the beginning of a major theological trajectory, to which Israel repeatedly returns.[8] In its hymns of praise Israel speaks *about God* in these terms, for example, Ps. 111:4-9 and 145:8-9. In its prayers of complaint, Israel speaks *to God* in these terms, urging God to act in ways consistent with this self-announcement, for example, Ps. 86:15. It is clear to Israel, here and subsequently, that this cluster of terms, given as divine oracle, provide the basis for life beyond the crisis. Israel will stake everything on its capacity and will to move beyond the disruption.

Yahweh's characteristic speech, however, is not yet finished. The oracle continues in v. 7b:

> . . .yet by no means clearing the guilty,
> but visiting the iniquity of the parents
> upon the children
> and the children's children,
> to the third and the fourth generation.

Yahweh is shown to be tough and unaccommodating. That also is given in the divine oracle. Thus the same Yahweh who in vv. 6-7a is so generously for Israel, in v. 7b is so ominously demanding and threatening against Israel.

Israel is not yet through the crisis, not yet assured of a future, because the very oracle that offers assurance, in the next breath takes away any certain assurance. It is no wonder that in vv. 8-9 Moses responds by promptly bowing toward the earth in worship, acting with profound deference. Moses offers a prayer that confesses the sin of Israel and seeks pardon for Israel:

> If now I have found favor in your sight, O Lord, I pray, let the Lord
> go with us. Although this is a stiff-necked people, pardon our iniq-
> uity and our sin, and take us for your inheritance.

It is as though Moses has spotted the deep contradiction between vv. 6-7a and v. 7b, and seeks assurance that Yahweh will act out of the great terms of fidelity in vv. 6-7a. In v. 10, Yahweh responds to Moses' passionate prayer, and agrees to be the faithful God of vv. 6-7a for Israel:

> I hereby make a covenant. Before all your people I will perform
> marvels, such as have not been performed in all the earth or in any
> nation; and all the people among whom you live shall see the work
> of the LORD; for it is an awesome thing that I will do with you.

Now, finally, after deep risk and danger, Israel is through the crisis and out of jeopardy. It is God's speech of faithfulness and steadfast love, of mercy and graciousness, of a promise of forgiveness, speech never before uttered, that is the basis of Israel's future with Yahweh and in the world. It is no surprise that this divine oracle emerges as a "characteristic speech" in Israel about God. The great words uttered (*rahum, hanun, hesed, 'emeth*) are embedded in a sentence attributed to Yahweh, situated in a divine oracle that serves as God's own announcement of God's self. Speech cannot become anymore elemental and primordial than this. And so we have a datum for Israel's "God talk," evoked in crisis, serving to resolve the crisis of broken covenant. Note well, that while v. 7b adds vocabulary that is threatening and dangerous, the option taken by Yahweh in v. 10 seems promptly to remove the statement of v. 7b from Israel's most characteristic speech.[9]

III

The second crisis I will consider is the collapse of the Northern Kingdom of Israel in 721 B.C.E. Unlike the Sinai tradition of Exodus 32–34, here we are on much firmer footing about the sociohistorical reality of the event. Israel's reflection, even though known primarily in the casting of Deuteronomic history, concerns a known, datable dynasty; a known, identifiable capitol city (Samaria); and a known, named political, military enemy, the empire of Assyria. The evidence of Israel's historiography, as well as evidence of the Assyrian annals, makes clear that this crisis in Northern Israel, culminating in 721 in the time of Sargon II, is a public crisis easily understood in terms of an expansive imperial policy and a recalcitrant would-be client state. The future of Israel as a kingdom in the north as a political entity is clearly quite uncertain and under threat.

Our notion of "crisis," however, requires along with this public, political dimension, also a theological dimension. This aspect of the crisis of 721 may not be visible to an outsider to Israel's faith. But we are here concerned with "insiders" who attend to the theological dimension of the public crisis, that is, who anticipate that the holiness of God is decisive even in matters that can be otherwise explained. For those "insiders," theological speech is not extrinsic to the event and its significance. "Crisis," as we are considering it, invites and requires "God-talk."

The text I shall consider, one of the most poignant in all of Israel's texts, is Hosea 2:2-23.[10] This poet-prophet of the eighth century, in a daring act of imagination, characterizes the public crisis of Israel in terms of the metaphor of marriage and divorce. It is not necessary to arrive at any critical conclusion concerning "Hosea's" personal experience or marriage, for we shall here treat it as a poetic metaphor.

The poem divides into two parts, and as David J. A. Clines has shown, the two parts are intimately and symmetrically related to each other.[11] The first part of the poem (vv. 2-13) concerns divorce, that is, the decision of the husband-Yahweh to divorce (abandon) the fickle wife-Israel. Thus the destruction of Israel wrought by the Assyrians is here understood poetically in terms of a violated theological-covenantal relationship, a violation that has inescapable worldly outcomes.[12] As we make a rough correlation between public event and poetic imagery the termination of North Israel in 721 is expressed by the end of v. 13 as the end of the marriage relationship.[13] Thus far into the poem, we are deep in the crisis. At v. 13, it is not known if there is any more future, indeed, if there is any more poem.

The first word of v. 14, "therefore" echoes the "therefore" of vv. 6 and 9. That term is characteristically used in prophetic speeches of judgment to mark the transition from indictment to sentence.[14] Thus, it most often bespeaks a threat from God as it does in vv. 6 and 9. After those two uses, we expect the third use in v. 14 to be one more intensification of threat and judgment. As we hear vv. 14-15, however, it is clear that there is a drastic and decisive turn in the poem, and therefore in the relationship voiced in the poem. Now, in contrast to vv. 2-13, there is talk of a "second entry" by Israel into the land of promise, because the first entry has been one of failure. Now the entry is to be one of hope, and therefore of new possibility:

> From there I will give her her vineyards,
>   and make the Valley of Achor a door of hope. (v. 15)

The wounded husband who has spoken in rejecting anger in vv. 2-13 now speaks in terms of pathos and possibility; as stated in v. 14, God now speaks "tenderly to her." As in Exod. 34:6-7, this poem is divine oracle. It is God's own speech into and through the crisis, a military crisis in Samaria, a covenantal crisis in the relationship between Yahweh and Israel. And as in Exod. 34:6-7, Yahweh must now speak as Yahweh has never spoken before. Yahweh now speaks words evoked, permitted, and required by the crisis that has endangered the relationship and that therefore endangers Israel's historical future as well.

This enraged husband now become wounded lover speaks of a new covenant with creation:

> I will make for you a covenant on that day with the wild animals, the birds of the air, and the creeping things of the ground. (v. 18a)[15]

Promptly after covenant with creation, this eager lover speaks of disarmament:

> I will abolish the bow, the sword, and war from the land; and I will make you lie down in safety. (v. 18b)

Then, in what appears to be the climactic statement of the entire poem, this speaker, now completely past the rage, voices a profound, positive intention:

> And I will take you for my wife forever; I will take you for my wife in righteousness and in justice, in steadfast love, and in mercy. I will take you for my wife in faithfulness; and you shall know the LORD. (2:19-20)

This remarkable statement on the lips of Yahweh is indeed a wedding vow. It is the promise of a husband to a new (reclaimed?) wife, vowing in extravagant, comprehensive language, full, complete, and abiding fidelity, the very fidelity that had been abandoned in vv. 2-13.

I suggest that it is these two verses in particular that are evoked by the crisis of brokenness, chronicled in vv. 2-13. It is these two verses especially that exhibit Yahweh speaking in and from, but also to and past the crisis. The events of 721 jeopardized Israel's covenant with Yahweh. In such jeopardy, Yahweh is driven to the most elemental speech of covenant fidelity that enables Israel to receive a future when external circumstance seem to preclude any such future.

The utterance of Yahweh in vv. 19-20 thus functions in the crisis of 721 quite like the utterance of Exod. 34:6-7 in the crisis of Sinai. For that reason, we may notice the ways in which Hosea 2:19-20 compares and contrasts with Exod. 34:6-7. First, we notice that three terms for fidelity, *ḥesed*, *raḥam*, *'amunah*, are reiterated, suggesting that these terms constitute Israel's core vocabulary for covenantal viability. But we also notice that this vow by Yahweh introduced two additional terms not present in the Sinai utterance, *ṣedeqah* and *mišpaṭ*, which, in many other places, constitute a major word pair in Israel's theological vocabulary.[16] Second, it is astonishing, but not to be taken for granted, that Hosea 2:19-20 has no negative counterpart as in Exod. 34:7b. The negativity about broken covenant is given full expression in Hosea 2:2-13, but has now been silenced and, we may assume, overcome in the theological process of the poem. Third, both the texts in Exod. 34:6-7 and Hosea 2:19-20 are divine oracles, first person utterances by Yahweh, and to that extent they are parallel in construction and intention.

It is also clear, however, that Hosea 2:19-20 has a dimension of passion and intensity not present in Exod. 34:6-7. In Exod. 34:6-7 Yahweh has declared in an objective and descriptive way that Yahweh's character is marked by fidelity. That notice of fidelity, however, is stated in an aloof manner, without any immediate commitment to Israel. This sense of reserve is reinforced by the negative counterpart of v. 7b.

In Hosea 2:19-20, by contrast, the recital of Yahweh's character as one of fidelity is in no way an objective or detached portrayal. That character is now expressed in terms of passionate commitment to Israel and determined intentionality to work a newness, with nothing kept back in reserve.[17] Thus, Hosea 2:19-20 stands closely related to Exod. 34:6-7 and is perhaps informed by it; but it also reflects a remarkable intensification of utterance. The negative of Exod. 34:7b has no counterpart in the poem

of Hosea 2. Instead, after 2:19-20 come vv. 21-23, which make clear that
the intimate, passionate, covenantal resolve of vv. 19-20 has large, public,
economic ramifications.

Again as in Exod. 34:6-7, in Hosea 2 the speech of Yahweh has been
evoked by the crisis, for never before has Yahweh spoken and committed
self with such unguarded passion. This self-commitment of Yahweh moves
against the threat of the crisis of 721 in order to assure Israel that it has a
future with Yahweh in the world.

The words of Israel's most characteristic speech have now in Hosea
2:19-20 emerged in a larger cluster. There are now five terms that portray
Yahweh's deep intention—*sedeqah, mišpat, hesed, raham,* and *'amunah.*
The words are embedded in a full sentence that not only characterizes the
personality of Yahweh, but also signals Yahweh's decisive, transformative
entry into this crisis of covenant. The words so embedded in a sentence of
intentionality are cast in the genre of divine oracle that takes the specific
form of vow. The dimension of passion has emerged as a much more powerful quality in Israel's most characteristic speech. One can sense in the second half of this long poem (vv. 14-23), that Yahweh has now extended self
to utter the most elemental speech possible, speech of self-commitment that
assures fidelity in a sociomilitary setting where nothing of fidelity appears
to endure. Israel's future may take a new form, no longer in an established
dynasty. On the basis of the assurance of a poetic-theological marriage
covenant metaphor, nonetheless, Israel has freedom, energy, and courage to
find alternative forms of existence in a situation marked by threat.

IV

The third crisis I will consider is inevitably the crisis of Judah's exile after
587 B.C.E., when the Babylonian armies effectively and harshly ended
Judah's established life in the environs of Jerusalem.[18] It is impossible to
overstate the depth of trauma produced in Jerusalem by the events of 587.[19]
There is no doubt that this was a public, political-military event of enormous public significance for Jews. At the same time, the textual material of
the Old Testament makes clear that this was a profound theological crisis
for Israel as well. Along with a deep sense of guilt articulated by the tradition of Deuteronomy, Israel was left with deep theological wonderment: Is
Yahweh any longer powerful (Isa. 50:2; 59:1)? Is Yahweh no longer faithful (Lam. 5:20; Isa. 49:14)? Is there indeed any future for this community
known by the name of Yahweh?

It is a most remarkable phenomenon, perhaps for ancient Israel a characteristic theological act, that the destabilization and displacement of 587
B.C.E. did not produce despair and resignation, though it did indeed produce deep grief.[20] Instead of despair and resignation, which would have

ended in silence, this profound crisis produced an amazingly rich and exten-
sive theological literature of a daring and venturesome kind. Indeed, the crisis of 587 is the clearest warrant for our contention that the crisis produces
speech, and the speech then turns to the resolution of the very crises which
evoked it.

While there are many texts that might be seen as evoked by the crisis of
exile and responding to the exile as a resolution, I will focus only upon Isa.
54:7-10 as one such text.[21] It will be clear to you why I focus on this text,
given its verbal affinities to Exod. 34:6-7 and Hosea 2:19-20. The larger
poem of Isaiah 54 is part of the corpus of Isaiah 40–55, the most eloquent
and imaginative assertion of Israel's future beyond exile. In Isaiah 54, the
poem takes up yet again the imagery of divorce that we have encountered
in Hosea 2.

In the imagery of Isaiah 54, Israel is like a humiliated woman.[22] The
"historical" context is that the community of Judeans is now shamed in the
eyes of the other, watching kingdoms, because Israel has trusted and served
a God who in 587 appears to these kingdoms to be weak, fickle, and ineffective. Israel's sense of communal humiliation in the exile is here expressed
by the poet as the humiliation of a woman. She is variously a barren woman
(54:1), a widow left in bereavement (54:4), and a woman rejected and
divorced (54:6-7). The imagery is not consistent and stable, but the con-
verging point of all of these images is unambiguous. A woman in that
ancient, patriarchal culture is honored by being married to a wealthy, powerful husband; conversely she is humiliated and made terribly vulnerable by
the loss of that relationship.[23] Rather than accenting the precise social role
to which she is assigned, what counts for the poet is her social situation of
humiliation.

After she is properly located and characterized, the husband speaks who
had abused and humiliated her, in this case, in exile:

> Do not fear, for you will not be ashamed;
>> do not be discouraged, for you will not suffer disgrace;
> for you will forget the shame of your youth,
>> and the disgrace of your widowhood you will remember no
>>> more.
> For your Maker is your husband (ba'al),
>> the LORD of hosts is his name. (Isa. 54:4-5a)

This remarkable statement has important links to Hosea 2, for in Hosea
2:16-17, the oracle asserts,

> On that day, says the LORD, you will call me "My husband," and
> no longer will you call me "My Baal." For I will remove the names
> of the Baals from her mouth, and they shall be mentioned by name
> no more.

Whereas the "husband" in Hosea 2 did not want to be *ba'al*, here in Isaiah 54, 200 years later Yahweh is the *ba'al*, the one who will make Israel pregnant with future.

After the shame of abandonment, now the husband is about to intervene and restore the relationship, as in Hosea 2:14-23. In this context, the restoration of relationship refers to restoration from exile to a good, joyous homecoming. But our text of focus is vv. 7-10. At the outset of these verses, we may notice an important difference between vv. 4-6 and vv. 7-10. Only in the latter verses does Yahweh speak directly in Yahweh's own voice, whereas in vv. 4-6, Yahweh is spoken of more distantly in the third person, while the poet describes and anticipates what Yahweh will do.

But now we come, yet a third time in our study, to a first person divine oracle, God's own speech, to the bereft, shamed woman. In vv. 7-8, we have one of the most remarkable theological assertions in all of the text of ancient Israel. In v. 7 and again in parallel fashion in v. 8, Yahweh concedes that Yahweh has caused the exile. Or in the language of the metaphor, Yahweh has initiated the humiliating separation, and Yahweh accepts responsibility for that separation:

> For a brief moment I abandoned you. . . .
> In overflowing wrath for a moment
>   I hid my face from you (Isa. 54:7a, 8a).

The governing verb, "I abandoned you" (*'azav*), is an honest acknowledgement that Yahweh perpetrated the divorce, as a husband could do in that ancient patriarchal society (see also Jer. 3:1). "For an instant," that is, for the space of a beat, Israel is cut off from Yahweh, the wife is denied access to her husband.[24] And in that instant, she is exposed, humiliated, and placed in terrible danger. The venturesome imagery is an act of candor, whereby the exile is given theological credence, without any hedging, denial, or explaining away.

Each of the acknowledgements in vv. 7a and 8a, however, is more than overcome by a powerful counterassertion, not unlike the assertion of Hosea 2:19-20:

> but with great compassion (*rahamim*) I will gather you . . . (v. 7b)
> but with everlasting love (*hesed*) I will have compassion (*raham*) on you, says the LORD, your Redeemer.[25] (v. 8b)

In these two verses, we have both a full acknowledgement of the crisis, a Yahweh-instituted theological crisis, and speech that resolved the crisis. In both lines, the term *rhm* occurs, here rendered "compassion," whereas in Exod. 34:6 and Hosea 2:19 the NRSV (which we have followed) rendered "mercy." The first use here is as a plural noun ("compassions"), and is reinforced in the second line by *hesed 'olam* ("everlasting love"), which functions as an adverbial clause modifying the verb, "have compassion."

While the grammar is more complicated, the speech that resolves the crisis includes two terms used in Exod. 34:6 and Hosea 2:19-20, *rhm* ("mercy, compassion") used twice, and *hesed* ("everlasting love, steadfast love"). Again the lines are cast as divine oracle. Yahweh speaks in order to move in, through, and beyond the crisis as in our other two cases. And as in the other two cases, Yahweh once again speaks as never before. The speech here is closely parallel to that of Hosea 2:19-20. It advances and intensifies beyond Hosea 2:19-20, however, so that Yahweh is able (forced to?) acknowledge, as is not done theretofore, Yahweh's initiation of the break in the relationship. This intensification bespeaks Yahweh's utter candor and full, passionate commitment to what is going on in the relationship, a relationship that is so yearned for and so problematic.

In vv. 9-10, the first person oracle continues, but with a slightly different focus. Now the first person speech of Yahweh makes a leap well beyond anything we have found in either Exod. 34:6-7 or Hosea 2:19-20. The oracle dares to suggest that the exile of Judah, that is, "this," is parallel to the "days of Noah," the flood of Gen. 6:5-9:17.[26] The leap is that the historical experience of exile is likened to the mythic portrayal of the cosmic event of flood.[27]

The connection to something of a cosmic dimension is not found at all in Exod. 34:6-7, though it is hinted at in Hosea 2:21-22, which moves toward the scope of all creation. The more dramatic, imaginative leap in Isaiah 54 may be the outcome of a different kind of traditioning process (that is, a royal trajectory), or it may be evoked by the severity of the crisis, whereby Jewish imagination is summoned into the larger arena of globalism. For whatever reason, this oracle of Yahweh takes in large scope the promise of v. 9, and like the promise in Gen. 8:21 and 9:15, is *after the crisis*, so that the crisis (flood, exile) will not happen again. The adverb "again" (*'odh*) occurs in all three statements of assurance:

> "I will never again (*'odh*) curse the ground because of humankind
> . . . nor will I ever again (*'odh*) destroy every living creature as I
> have done." (Gen. 8:21)

> ". . . never again (*'odh*) shall all flesh be cut off by the waters of a
> flood, and never again (*'odh*) shall there be a flood to destroy the
> earth." (Gen. 9:11)

> Just as I swore that the waters of Noah
> would never again (*'odh*) go over the earth,
> so I have sworn that I will not be angry with you
> and will not rebuke you. (Isa. 54:9)

Verse 10 takes up the sweeping parallelism proposed in v. 9 and relates it directly to the now familiar vocabulary of covenantal fidelity. What will not depart (*muš*) or be removed (*mot*) is "my steadfast love (*hesed*), "my covenant of peace" (*berith šalom*), promises the God of "compassion" (*raham*). As in the other texts we have considered, the crisis of exile evokes a divine oracle built around the primary words of Israel's God-talk. There is again a triad of important terms. Two of them, *hesed* and *raham*, we have also noted in Exod. 34:6, Hosea 2:19-20, and more immediately in Isa. 54:7-8. These terms recur in texts asserting the constancy of Yahweh in the face of crisis and discontinuity.

The third term in this triad, "covenant of peace," we have not before encountered in our study.[28] The phrasing occurs elsewhere only in Ezek. 34:25 and 37:26; thus it is peculiarly an exilic usage. That is, it is a powerful promise matching in scope and intensity the scope and intensity of the exilic crisis. In Ezek. 34:25, the *berith shalom* makes it possible to dwell "securely," even in the face of "wild animals" (vv. 25, 28). In Ezek. 37:26, the *berith shalom* is said to be an "everlasting covenant" (*berith olam*), thereby connecting our passage to those concerning the long-term durability of the relationship, a durability not to be disrupted by any crisis. Thus in Isa. 54:10 the *berith shalom* is understood to be "everlasting," i.e., it will persist even when the mountains and hills, that is, the sure structures of creation, are destabilized. (The same assertion in different language is evident in Jer. 31:35-36, 37).

V

My argument intends to show that Israel's "most characteristic speech" in times of crisis is speech that gathers around this poignant and peculiar cluster of words. We have examined three crises—the violation of covenant at Sinai, the fall of the Northern Kingdom, and the exile of the sixth century—each of which placed the future of Israel in jeopardy. We have found that in each of these crises, Israel is the recipient of a divine oracle from the very lips of God.

We have seen first of all, that the words used in these divine oracles are fairly constant, constant enough to permit a generalization. The two words that recur in all three texts are *hesed* and *raham*. Along with them, the terms are distributed as follows:

- Exod. 34:6-7a *rhm, hnn, 'rk 'ppym, hsd, 'mth, hsd*
- Hosea 2:19-20 *sdq, mšpt, hsd, rhmm, 'munh*
- Isa. 54:10 *hsd, brth, šlm, rhm*

With different nuances, all of these terms bear witness to God's constancy for the relationship, a constancy rooted only in God's intentionality, a constancy so resolved that it will not be disrupted from the other side, that is, due to the conduct or stance of Israel.

Second, we have noticed in these three oracles an intensification of God's passionate commitment. In Exod. 34:6-7a, Yahweh only disclosed God's self in a relatively detached way. This is how God is! In Hosea 2:19-20, God takes an active role in reestablishing a broken relationship; but in Hosea 2:2-13, Israel is clearly the one responsible for the failure of the relationship. But in Isa. 54:7-10, Yahweh acknowledges God's own part in the failure of the relationship, for it is Yahweh, the husband, who has terminated the relationship, at least "for a moment." This candor and passion in Isa. 54:7-10 is a far cry from the cold symmetry of Exod. 34:6-7a, as Yahweh has become increasingly drawn into Israel's life. That is, Yahweh seems to care more about the relationship than is evident in Exod. 34:6-7.

I wish to draw from these reflections three conclusions. The first is in the form of a question: Does God's fidelity to Israel exist prior to the crisis and persist through the crisis, or does God's fidelity arise in always deeper ways only in the midst of the crisis? The question may seem to be a rather subtle point, but it concerns the dramatic dynamic of Israel's faith, and we may say, the dynamic character of the God of Israel. It is an easier and more conventional judgment to say that the God of Israel has always been such a God of constancy, always characterized by these recurring modifiers, always prepared to be faithful to Israel.

I am inclined, however, to argue the more difficult case, namely, that God's fidelity to Israel arises in greater and more intense measure only in and through the crisis, so that even Yahweh's own predilection toward Israel is in important ways context driven. Thus I am inclined to approach these texts with a good deal of theological "realism," of a rather naïve kind, to entertain the notion that Israel understands that something decisive happens to Yahweh in and through the drama of the text.[29] It is clear in Exod. 34:6-7, where Yahweh states the two-sided options available to God, that only in v. 10, in response to the prayer of Moses in vv. 8-9, does Yahweh determine to enact the fidelity asserted in vv. 6-7a. It may be agreed that this inordinate fidelity is available as potential in vv. 6-7a, but it is not concretely enacted until v. 10, as though Yahweh in this moment, in response to Moses, makes a new decision not ever before made.

In a similar way, in the poem of Hosea 2, Yahweh does an about face after v. 13.[30] In vv. 2-13, Yahweh has been angry and unqualified in the rejection of Israel as spouse. Whatever one makes of the relationship of the two parts of the poem, as the larger poem now stands, something decisive happens to Yahweh after v. 13 that had not happened to Yahweh before this moment of deep crisis, a crisis that is historical-military as well as covenantal. It is most plausible to suppose that it is the very depth of the crisis, evidenced in the rage that rejects Israel as spouse, which moves Yahweh to reverse field and to make a vigorous effort to reestablish the relationship.[31]

The case is not different in Isaiah 54. Indeed, Yahweh acknowledged that "for a moment" "overflowing wrath" did prevail and cause rejection. The poem and the future of Israel are reversed because of great compassion and everlasting love. It is clear, however, that Yahweh's great compassion and everlasting love were not active or available until the crisis of exile evoked Yahweh's new resolve. Unless one wants to imagine that Yahweh is a manipulator who loves but also withholds love (which seems to me a more problematic theological judgment), it is most plausible to conclude that it is precisely the crisis that evokes Yahweh's deep love, as it evokes Yahweh's speech that was not on the horizon (even on God's horizon?) until the crisis.

Thus, Yahweh stands vulnerable, exposed to, and impinged upon by the power and depth of the crisis. It is, in my judgment, the anguish and loss linked to the rejection of Israel-Judah that summons Yahweh to new dimensions of fidelity that were not heretofore entertained, either by Israel, or by the poet, or even by Yahweh.

In turn, it is the speech of Yahweh that in its very utterance resolves the crisis. That is, it resolves the theological-covenantal crisis. Israel believes the utterance also is the beginning point of resolving the political-military crisis that in each case besets Israel. When Yahweh speaks in Exod. 34:10, the threat of a nullified covenant is ended. In Hosea 2:19-20, the vow of remarriage ends the decree of divorce. In Isa. 54:10, the utterance of promise overcomes the deep shame of rejection. To be sure, the triumph of fidelity in each case concerns the theological existence of Israel-Judah, and does not directly comment upon the sociopolitical future of Israel. In Israel's imagination, however, such theological impingement cannot be kept from making a decisive difference in Israel's and Judah's public circumstance.

Second, I propose that the vocabulary and form of utterance in these three uses are not isolated cases or incidental transactions in Israel's life with Yahweh. Rather they are characteristic of that relationship. That is, these texts (and many others that seem related to or derived from them) embody a major motif in Israel's discernment of Yahweh and of life with Yahweh. Against the exploitative power of the great empires of Egypt, Assyria, and Babylon, and against the seductive social practices of "Canaanites," Israel arrives at the conviction and judgment that covenantal fidelity is at the core of reality, theological and social. Israel employs this recurring vocabulary in every facet of its speech and reflection, in order to characterize not only its expectation of Yahweh, but also to voice its intention for social relations.

It is this affirmation and embrace of covenantal fidelity that haunts Israel's socioeconomic, political practice as is evident in its laws. And it is this same affirmation and embrace that causes Israel's life with Yahweh to be saturated with justice questions that eventually culminate in issues of theodicy. Thus we are here at the voicing of the major issues that preoccupy Israel's thought and imagination.

Third, it is my suggestion that this "most characteristic speech" about fidelity that is rooted in heaven and extends its reach into the earth is a major contribution to the life and discourse of our contemporary society. This God-talk (which eventuates in a different kind of neighbor-talk) stands in stark contrast to and as a powerful challenge against the primary speech forms and social relationships of our culture.

Against the claims of covenantal fidelity, our society is greatly tempted to autonomy, commoditization, and reduction of all of life to the technical. I use these terms to refer in turn to: a) *autonomy* as the "possessive individualism" of consumerism, whereby each is presented as an autonomous agent without definitional connectedness to any other, and who thereby is free to order life without any abiding loyalty or defining commitment;[32] b) *commoditization* as the propensity to regard everything, including neighbor and self, as objects to be managed, manipulated, and exploited, without any recognition of the mystery of "Thouness" that properly belongs to self and to other; and c) *reduction to the technical* as the manipulation of the advantages of power and knowledge, without any thought of value or worth that might limit or direct technical power and technical capacity. It is clear that where covenantal fidelity is nullified in the interest of these modes of life, something deathly happens to all parties—the strong and the weak. Thus, the pertinence of biblical shapings of reality and of language has not to do with the maintenance of a class morality or of instrumental privilege, nor of cultural advantage of the "Christian West." Its pertinence, rather, is a vision of where reality is centered (God-talk), and of how social power is to be trusted, respected, and deployed among those who practice fidelity toward each other.

I believe that the recovery of the "most characteristic speech" of ancient Israel is not simply an in-house gain for scripture study or for the religious communities adhering to the Hebrew Bible. Rather such recovery matters for the larger public conversation in which biblical discernments of reality can play a part. It is my judgment that finding a proper form for Old Testament Theology (Biblical Theology) must in part be concerned with the certitudes of "God-talk." It must at the same time, however, attend to the larger public crises of life and death, for biblical speech characteristically arises in and for such crises.

VI

Finally I will mention three other texts that embody Israel's response to the divine oracles we have already considered. It is methodologically important that Israel first of all *hears* these characterizations of Yahweh in the form of divine oracle. It is equally important that this affirmation of God's fidelity then moves from the lips of Yahweh (and the ears of Israel) to the mouth of Israel to become Israel's own affirmation that redefines the life of Israel, even as the oracles have recharacterized the life of Yahweh.

1. The best known and perhaps most important use of this "characterization of Yahweh" is on the lips of Moses in Num. 14:18-19. In the larger narrative of Numbers 14, Israel characteristically complains and resists (vv. 2-4, 10), and Yahweh is so provoked that Yahweh proposes to Moses to destroy Israel (vv. 11-12).

Between complaining Israel and provoked Yahweh, Moses intervenes to petition Yahweh. Moses acts as Yahweh's theological instructor.[33] Moses explains that while Yahweh is within propriety to destroy recalcitrant Israel, the foreign kingdoms will misconstrue such an action and conclude that Yahweh "is not able to bring this people into the land he swore to give them." That is, Yahweh's act of anger will be taken by the foreign kingdoms as a sign of Yahweh's weakness and failure.

Moses urges Yahweh to an alternative action. Moses' urging, voiced in vv. 17-19, is a speak-back of Exod. 34:6-7. That is, Moses remembers what Yahweh has said in that oracle and says it back to Yahweh. Moses holds Yahweh to Yahweh's own resolve to be "steadfast and forgiving," and on that basis petitions for forgiveness. Moses engages in Yahweh's "most characteristic speech," which Yahweh in turn finds compelling. Thus, Yahweh's self-disclosure becomes the basis for a persuasive petition to Yahweh.

2. This same vocabulary figures powerfully in the center of the lamentation over fallen Jerusalem (Lam. 3:22-24). The Book of Lamentations is for the most part an unrelieved song of grief over destroyed Jerusalem, the same crisis to which Isa. 54:7-10 addresses itself. The poetry of these five poems is relentless in its honesty about loss. The most prominent exception to that sense of loss is in 3:22-24, almost midpoint in the collection.

In 3:18, the poet asserts,

> I say, "Gone is my glory,
>   and all that I had hoped (yḥl) for from the LORD."

But then, as an answer to the loss of hope, the speaker engages in an act of remembering:

> But this I call to mind,
>   and therefore I have hope (yḥl). (v. 21)

The loss of hope was the result of focusing too singularly on the present moment of defeat. An act of memory enables the speaker to look away from this defeat, in order to draw upon older, continuing resources. And this is what is remembered:

> Yahweh's mercy (ḥsd) is surely not at an end
>   nor is his pity (rḥm) exhausted.
> It is new every morning. Great is your faithfulness ('munh)!
> Yahweh is my portion, I tell myself, therefore I will hope
> (yḥl). (3:22-24)[34]

The same word, "hope," (*yḥl*) is used three times, concerning a loss of hope (v. 18), a resolve to hope (v. 21), and as a conclusion of hope (v. 24).

What makes hope possible is the reiteration and recital of the triad *ḥesed*, *raḥam*, and *'amunah*, terms we have seen in the three divine oracles we have considered. Indeed, Kraus notes the links of our passage to Isa. 54:10 with the same terminology.[35] The recall of the divine oracle of self-disclosure permits the griever for a moment to redefine the situation of despairing Jerusalem. Thus the divine oracle becomes the basis for a practice of quite concrete, crisis-situated hope, for the triad from the self-disclosure of Yahweh recharacterizes the crisis.

3. Finally, I mention Psalm 85:8-13. While Num. 14:18 and Lam. 3:20-22 are from "the human side," that is, uttered as a human statement, these verses are commonly regarded as a "prophetic oracle" issued in worship, that is, "from God's side."[36] I list these verses in my second group of texts because they are not presented as a "divine oracle" from God's mouth. They are at best mediated through a human speaker who operates as a cultic functionary. That is, even if they purport to be a reassurance from God about ultimate well-being, they are spoken by a human person who appeals to the already extant divine oracles. This does not place the verses "on the human side," but they are a later use of the older tradition of oracle.

Verse 8 supports the scholarly opinion that this is a prophetic speaker whom Kraus refers to as a "shalom prophet":[37]

> Let me hear what God the LORD will speak,
>   for he will speak peace to his people.

That is, the whole of the message is *shalom*, comprehensive well-being. Note that this is the word used in Isa. 54:10, *berith shalom*, "covenant of peace."

In vv. 10-13 our familiar cluster of terms recurs as a promise of the complete establishment of the good rule of Yahweh, that is, the "kingdom of God." The promise appears to be spoken in response to a complaint concerning exile, so that again, we have a stylized example of speech arising from and responding to crisis. In this case, the terms we have taken as modifiers now become something like personified agents of God's new age.

> Steadfast love (*ḥsd*) and faithfulness (*mt*) will meet;
>   righteousness (*ṣedeq*) and peace (*šalom*) will kiss each
>   other.
> Faithfulness (*mt*) will spring up from the ground,
>   and righteousness (*ṣedeq*) will look down from the sky.
> The Lord will give what is good (*ṭov*),
>   and our land will yield its increase.
> Righteousness (*ṣedeq*) will go before him,
>   and will make a path for his steps. (vv. 10-13)

There will be a convergence of all of these powers of fidelity meeting, kissing, coming together from the ground and from the sky, so that all things will cohere. The consequence of this convergence will be a productive, prosperous, food-producing earth. All creation will be its true self.[38] Weiser, with his propensity to link everything to Sinai, sees that this passage appeals to Exod. 34:6 and on the renewal of creation to Hosea 2:21-22, just after the marriage vow that we have considered.[39]

Thus the divine oracle, rooted in crisis, eventuates in a profound act of hope for a time when God's way will be effective in all of creation. In every crisis, Israel holds to these old and characteristic self-offers of Yahweh, and so transposes the crises into a caring future that will overcome and defeat every unbearable present tense. If the crisis generates despair, Israel's speech, rooted in God's speech, takes the side of confident hope.

VII

I conclude with the use made of Psalm 85 by Isak Dinesen in *Babette's Feast*. In the tale, Lorens Loewenhielm is situated in two scenes related to Psalm 85. In the first scene, he appears as a normal young man. He sees Martine and is smitten. The narrator observes:

> Young Lorens till now had not been aware of any particular spiritual gift in his own nature. But at this one moment there rose before his eyes a sudden, mighty vision of a higher and purer life, with no creditors, dunning letters or parental lectures, with no secret, unpleasant pangs of conscience and with a gentle, golden-haired angel to guide and reward him.[40]

He goes to her house, meets her father, the intimidating Dean. In her presence, he is tongue-tied. The father seizes his pause to assert,

> Mercy and Truth, dear brethren, have met together . . .
> Righteousness and Bliss have kissed one another.

The narrator adds to the words of the father,

> And the young man's thoughts were with the moment when Lorens and Martine should be kissing each other.[41]

> But then he abruptly departs, because he senses his own inadequacy. I shall never, never see you again! For I have learned here that Fate is hard, and that in this world there are things which are impossible![42]

But he does see Martine again. In his second scene with her, Lorens returns now in his older years, fully prosperous and successful, seasoned and mature. He sees Martine again in her loveliness. After he has eaten and drunk his fill, he makes a speech:

> Mercy and truth, my friends, have met together . . .
> Righteousness and bliss shall kiss one another . . .

> We tremble before making our choice in life, and after having made it again tremble in fear of having chosen wrong. But the moment comes when our eyes are opened, and we see and realize that grace is infinite. Grace, my friends, demands nothing from us but that we shall await it and confidence and acknowledge it in gratitude. Grace, brothers, makes no conditions and singles out none of us in particular; grace takes us all to its bosom and proclaims general amnesty. See! that which we have chosen is given us, and that which we have refused is, also and at the same time, granted us. Ay, that which we have rejected is poured upon us abundantly. For mercy and truth have met together, and righteousness and bliss have kissed one another.[43]

His listeners know that they have been led to a moment of truth: "They had been given one hour of the millennium."[44] As Lorens left, he said to Martine, his ancient love, "For tonight I have learned, dear sister, that in this world anything is possible." You remember that in his first sad leaving, he had said, "I have learned here that Fate is hard, and that in this world there are things which are impossible." Now, in his second leaving, he affirms, "I have learned, dear sister, that in this world anything is possible." And Martine responds, "Yes, it is so, dear brother, . . . In this world anything is possible."[45]

Dinesen has moved a long way from the prophetic oracle of Psalm 85, which had already moved a long distance from the terror of Mt. Sinai voiced in Exod. 34:6-7. All of these texts and all of their readings, however, hold a common theme. They assert that in a world of fidelity, everything is made possible by the faithful one. Israel refuses infidelity as a norm of life, and refuses along with that refusal, to accept Hard Fate which makes things impossible. The God of fidelity continues to open what the world regards as closed. Such "characteristic speech" generates buoyant hope and trust that is durable, persistent, and demanding.

9

The Role of Old Testament Theology in Old Testament Interpretation

WHILE OLD TESTAMENT THEOLOGY MAY BE SAID TO HAVE SOMETHING OF a constant and recurrent role in Scripture study, it is important to recognize that the particular impact and responsibility of theological interpretation on the larger field of study varies greatly, depending upon interpretive context and the questions mediated in specific cultural contexts.

I

It is possible to distinguish in scholarship four rather distinctive phases of critical study, each of which hosted theological interpretation in a way peculiar to its horizon. The following is a summary of those phases:

1. *The Reformation Period.* It was in the Reformation that "biblical theology" became a distinct enterprise, as theological interpretation was undertaken apart from the sacramental system of the church and to some extent outside the conventional categories of the dogmatic tradition.[1] In that context, "biblical theology" had as its role the attempt to voice the fresh, free, live word of gospel, completely uncontained and unfettered by any hegemonic categories of established church tradition. Different traditions in the Reformation, of course, gave different accents to this newly "evangelical" interpretation, best known in Lutheran *grace* and Calvinistic *sovereignty*. In all these cases, however, the effort was made to deal directly with "the things of God" in the text, without mediating forms and structures that worked toward domestication and containment. Thus "biblical theology" had a distinctly evangelical impetus.

2. *Enlightenment Historicism.* While the forms and cadences of Reformation "biblical theology" persisted into the seventeenth century, the notion of unfettered witness to the things of God was exceedingly difficult to maintain. In both Lutheran and Calvinist circles (not to speak at all of Trent), the great claims of unfettered gospel were eventually reduced to new scholastic formulation, surely as domesticated as the scholastic formulations against which the primal Reformers had worked.[2]

In that context, the move from *dogmatic* to *historical* questions was an attempt to emancipate biblical interpretation from the deep domestication of Scripture. It is exceedingly important to recall that the emergence and appropriation of "the historical" was an effort to maintain the free availability of scriptural claims against the new theological scholasticism. It is common to cite the lecture of Johann Philip Gabler in 1797 as the decisive articulation of this new approach, whereby Gabler insisted that Old Testament study was primarily a historical and not dogmatic enterprise.[3] As Ben Ollenburger has shown, however, Gabler's intention is more subtle than the simple categories of dogmatic–historical may indicate.[4]

Focus upon "the historical" brought with it the subsequently developed notion of "God acts in history." But the primary energy released by this new category was devoted to historical *criticism* and the effort to situate every text according to its date and recoverable context. This movement culminated in Wellhausen's great synthesis that is aptly entitled *Prolegomena to the History of Israel*.[5] That is, the documentary hypothesis, for which Wellhausen is widely credited and blamed, is a preparation for doing *history*.

Historical criticism, perhaps inevitably, focused upon the history of Israelite religion, thus situating each religious practice and implied theological claim in a specific context, understanding each practice and claim as context specific. The outcome was to relativize every practice and claim, to permit a developmental scheme by which every practice and claim was eventually displaced (superseded!) by another. As a consequence, every practice and claim is pertinent only to its immediate historical context. In that enterprise, which stretches, as we conveniently put it, from Gabler to Wellhausen, the study of the history of Israelite religion almost completely displaced Old Testament theology, the latter continued only in a subdued way as a rearguard action to maintain the "constancies" of "orthodoxy." It is of particular interest that whereas biblical theology in the Reformation period was emancipatory, in the period of high Enlightenment it was, where it was undertaken at all, not so much emancipatory as conserving and consolidating, an attempt to resist the vigorous enterprise of relativizing historicism. Such an approach to the text was distinctly against the spirit of the times.

3. *The Barthian Alternative.* The dominance of a history of religions approach, with its relativizing consequence, inevitably evoked a response. But no one could have imagined that the response would be as forceful, bold, and demanding as that offered by Karl Barth in his commentary on Romans (*Römerbrief*) in 1919.[6] Barth's effort was to interpret the text in a boldly and unembarrassedly theological, normative way, without yielding anything to historical relativism and without reducing faithful practice and theological claim to contextual explanation.

It is difficult to overstate the decisive contribution of Barth in turning the interpretive enterprise and in freshly validating theological interpretation that dared to treat theological claim in the text as constant and normative. Barth enlivened and legitimated nearly a century of theological interpretation, including the most important work in Old Testament theology; but of course from the perspective of scholars who, for personal or intellectual reasons, fear and resist such claims of the "normative," Barth is to be regarded as an unfortunate digression in the discipline.

While Barth's theological eruption already in 1919 is taken as a decisive break in Enlightenment historicism, it is not possible to appreciate the impact of Barth apart from the later context of his work, with particular reference to the challenge of National Socialism in Germany and the articulation of the Barmen Declaration in 1934. The mood and tenor of the work is profoundly *confessional,* an assertion of *normative* truth that had practical consequences and that implied personal and concrete risk. That mood and tenor of confession did not bother to make itself persuasive to "cultural despisers" who, by historical criticism, managed to tone down evangelical claims for God to make matters compatible with Enlightenment reason. The daring claims made in a Barthian posture stand in deep contrast with the consolidating, even reactionary function of biblical theology in the earlier period of historicism. Barth's dominance is a prime example of the ways in which context presents questions and challenges that push biblical theology in one direction rather than another. It is unmistakable that the crisis of the twentieth century both required and permitted biblical theology in ways neither permitted nor required in the earlier period of high historicism.

The legacy of Barth may be said to have dominated the field of biblical theology until about 1970. In the center of that period is the magisterial work of Walther Eichrodt, who took *covenant* as his mode of normativeness, and the even more influential work of Gerhard von Rad, whose definitive essay of 1938 surely echoes the credo-orientation of Barmen.[7] While the normativeness and constancy of Barth's perspective can take different forms, both Eichrodt and von Rad sought to provide a place of normativeness in which to stand in the face of the huge barbarisms of the twentieth century, for it was clear that the domestications of historical criticism provided no standing ground at all. More than Eichrodt, von Rad continued to attend to and be puzzled by the unmistakable dynamic of historical change reflected in the faith of Israel, but he finally does not yield to it. In the United States, moreover, the odd juxtaposition of normative theological claim and historical vagary was handled with remarkable finesse and, for the moment, in a compelling way by G. Ernest Wright in his influential *God Who Acts.*[8]

It is to be noticed that while this essentially Barthian enterprise of "the Short Century" might provide credible ground for faith midst the brutalities of history, it is also the case that the interpretive movement out of Barth was vigorously hegemonic, providing in various ways a summary account of the faith of ancient Israel that was exclusionary in its claims and allowed little room for alternative reading.[9] While such an assertiveness can well be understood in the context of brutality whereby interpretation was an emergency activity, it is also important to recognize that such a hegemonic posture evokes an inescapable response at the end of its domination, a response of considerable force and authority.

4. *The Coming of Postmodernity*. It is now common to cite 1970 as the break point of what came to be called (pejoratively) "The Biblical Theology Movement," that interpretive enterprise propelled by Barth and especially voiced by von Rad and Wright. The "ending" of that monopolistic interpretive effort was occasioned by many factors. It is conventional to cite the work of Brevard Childs and James Barr as the decisive voices of the ending, even though it is clear that Barr and Childs come from very different directions and agree on almost nothing except their critique.[10] Also to be fully appreciated, from inside the movement itself, is the insistence of Frank Moore Cross (colleague of Wright) that Israel is enmeshed in ancient Near Eastern culture and is not as distinctive as had been urged, and of Claus Westermann (colleague of von Rad), who urged that the horizon of creation was as important as the "historical recital" for the faith of Israel.[11]

More broadly, since 1970 the rise of feminist and liberation hermeneutics and the failure of mono-interpretation have produced an interpretive context that is by many styled "postmodern," that is, after the hegemony that had dominated the twentieth century.[12] Coming to the more important features of this development of scholarship that has put the work of Old Testament theology in some disarray, we may notice three:

• *Pluralism*. Von Rad has already taken seriously the pluralism of the theological claims of the Old Testament text. But now the awareness of pluralism is much deeper and more seriously noticed, so that the text seems to admit of no single, grand formulation. Indeed not only does the text offer a plurality of God-claims, but when read closely, the several texts themselves are plurivocal, open to a variety of readings. The quality and character of the text, moreover, is matched increasingly by a plurality of readers, reflecting a diverse community of interests, so that no single synthetic reading is any longer possible.[13]

• *Ideology*. It follows from a full-faced acknowledgement of pluralism, that one can readily see that every offer of normativeness is in some sense ideology. Most benignly this means it is an advocacy for a certain perspective and not a given. Thus, even the hegemonic approach held in common by Barth, Eichrodt, von Rad, and Wright is seen to be not as a stable foundation, but rather an advocacy on offer to the larger interpretive community that must be received and adjudicated by interpreters who occupy other ideological perspectives.[14] Behind this collage of interpretive adjudications among advocacies, we are able to see more clearly that the pluralism in the text itself concerns the things of God, a collage of competing advocacies that made it into the text, advocacies that are not done (we may assume) in bad faith, but that are not easily or quietly compatible.

• *Speech as constitutive*. Emphasis upon the power of rhetoric, when considered in the context of pluralism and ideology, makes clear that speech about God is not simply reportage on "what happened" in history or "what is" in ontology, but the speech itself is as powerfully constitutive of theological claim as it is of historical "past."[15] Thus the new, postmodern world of theological interpretation is powerfully focused on utterance—a concrete utterance offered in the text and an *interpretive utterance* offered in contemporary conversation. Insofar as utterance is taken as mere utterance, it may indeed be shaped either by the dogmatic claims of the ecclesial community or by the requirements of Enlightenment reason. But it is also in the very character of utterance that it may be a *novum*, which can be recognized in some quarters as a claim of truth beyond the fetters of church or academy.[16] Thus it is *the appropriation and reception of utterance* and *the critique of utterance* that I take to be the work of Old Testament theology. In our present context, this reception, appreciation, and critique of utterance takes place in the loud and dissonant presence of many voices. But this accent on utterance as the offer of new truth also has important continuities with the Reformation accent upon the word and with the insistence of Barth, even though that appreciation, reception, and critique must now be done in a quite different form.

II

The location of Old Testament theology in a postmodern situation sets some severe limits on what is possible but also yields some legitimate place for such demanding, important work. Both the severe limits and the legitimate place, however, are freshly situated in a new cultural, interpretive context in which old practices must indeed be relinquished. Indeed, the case is readily made that from our present vantage point (that also must not be absolutized as has been a recurring temptation for every vantage point), Old Testament theology has been much too often imperialistically Christian, coercively moralistic, and vigorously anti-Semitic.[17] These critiques of past work must be taken seriously and count much more, in my judgment, than the easier contention that theological interpretation does not honor Enlightenment rationality and is therefore fideistic.

Old Testament theology in such a context, I propose, may have the following marks:[18]

• *"Theo-logy"* is "speech about God." That is, it does not concern, in any primary sense, all that might be said of Israel's religion, but it is an attempt to pay attention to the God who emerges in the utterance of these texts, a God marked by some constancy, but a God given in a peculiar, even scandalous characterization. Whatever else may be said of this God, it is clear that the God of the Old Testament conforms neither to conventional monotheism nor to flat dogmatic categories, nor to usual philosophical Enlightenment assumptions of the West, though it is equally clear that a monotheizing tendency is at work.[19]

• *Speech about God* is given by human persons, reflected in human institutions and in human contexts, serving human, political agendas. This is no new insight and no threat to the enterprise. All the efforts to minimize "the historical," moreover, cannot eliminate the fact that human persons have done these utterances. Thus the God of Israel is given us *on the lips of Israel,* constituted through utterance—utterance no doubt deeply driven and informed by lived experience but in the end shaped by artistic, imaginative utterance.

• Such speech about God is not idle chatter but is characteristically *intentional speech* and is so treated in the canonizing process. More specifically, we may say that *intentional human speech about God* is *testimony,* an attempt to give a particular account of reality with this God as agent and as character at its center.[20] And while we may notice the great pluralism in the text in God-utterances, we may also, perhaps more importantly, observe a family kinship of all these utterances when set over against alternative accounts of reality, ancient or modern. While close theological reading will attend to the differences in utterance, Old Testament theology in the end has a propensity toward that shared kinship, to see what is recurring midst the vagaries of testimony.

• Old Testament theology treats of the *text of canon* and so takes *human testimony* as *revelation.*[21] One need not so take it, and many scholars preoccupied with historical questions would not make that move, even though what is claimed to be "history" turns out almost every time to be advocacy. Be that as it may, Old Testament theology, in its attention to what is recurring and constant in Israel's God-utterance, takes that God-utterance to be *disclosing.* I understand, of course, that the history of Christian revelation, with its deposit of dogmatic truth, has been profoundly coercive; here I use "revelatory" and "disclosing" to mean that the God-utterance of Israel seeks to *un-close* lived reality that without the generative force of Yahweh as character and agent is characteristically *closed* in ways of denial, despair, and/or oppression.

• To take Israel's God-speech as revelatory means to view it as utterance that seeks to speak about a *mystery* attending to and dwelling in the world in which Israel lives. That mystery, according to Israel's utterance, is on the loose, wild and dangerous, often crude, inaccessible, unattractive, capable of violence, and equally capable of positive transformation.[22] In its God-speech Israel does not set out everywhere to give us an attractive or appealing God, the stable God of church catechism or the winsome God of therapeutic culture. But it does seek to give an account of an agency of *otherness* who operates with intentional purpose and who refuses to be captive either to slogans of self-sufficiency or in the terminology of despair.[23]

Israel's God-speech seeks to give an account of restless holiness that decisively redefines and resituates everything else about life.

• Israel's God-speech, moreover, in a rich variety of ways, offers that this Other is *provisionally identifiable.* God in the Old Testament is identifiable, known by characteristic actions that are recognizable from one context to another, known by direct utterance treasured and passed on, known by moves that can be placed in the text and on the lips of the witnesses. Because that Other is genuinely *other,* however, Israel itself knows that all such identification is provisional and not final or certain.[24] And so there are "many names," many metaphors and images, many songs, poems, and narratives, all of which attest differently.[25] There are crises of naming when the name is displaced (Exod. 3:14; 6:2), and there is a withholding of the name (Gen. 32:29).[26] In the end, moreover, there is the inscrutability of the Tetragrammaton (YHWH), Israel's final resistance to idolatry and Israel's defiant notice to check both church theologians who know too much about this Other and academic theologians who work apart from this Other.

• In a postmodern context, it is important to accept that these voices of God-talk are all advocates in the debate about how to voice provisional identity of the undoubted, unaccommodating Other. Thus "J," 2 Isaiah, Job, and Ezra each advocate differently. At the most they advocate, but they do not finally know. They are *witnesses* and neither judge nor jury.[27] They propose and offer but do not finally comprehend. Insofar as all these witnesses agree (which is not very far), their shared utterance is also advocacy and not certitude. In our postmodern context, it can hardly be more than advocacy.

I am, however, quick to insist that there are many scholars who discount the God-speech of Israel in the name of "disinterested" scholarship, who refuse theological questions on the ground of "history," who are themselves advocates and not more than advocates.[28] We have arrived at the odd situation in which the *resisters* to the God-utterances of Israel posture themselves as more certain than the *practitioners* of Old Testament theology dare to be; but in fact the resisters also are only advocates of Enlightenment rationality, bespeaking old and long wounds from ancient theological coerciveness, preferring a self-contained, self-explanatory world to one of hurt-producing theological authoritarianism. A postmodern Old Testament theology, so it seems to me, dare not be coercive and need not be coercive. For in our present context, Old Testament theology is proposal and not conclusion, offer and not certainty. Interpretation stands always in front of our deciding and not after. For the *otherness* of reality given us on the lips of Israel makes our deciding always penultimate and provisional, always yet again unsettled by new disclosings.

III

Given the history of the discipline, and given a postmodern situation with
no agreed-upon "meta-narrative,"[29] we may now consider the role of Old
Testament theology in the discipline, a role that must respect both the critical foundations of the discipline and the postmodern options that at the
same time limit and permit.

I purpose that the primal role of Old Testament theology is to attend to
the testimony out of which lived reality was then and may now be reimagined with reference to a Holy Character who is given us on the lips of Israel,
who exhibits some constancy, but whose constancy is regularly marked by
disjunction and tension.[30] The act of *imagining alternatively* is what these
witnesses are doing in the text-world itself, and the on-going option of
imagining alternatively is kept alive by continual attentiveness to this testimony.[31] That Holy Character on the lips of the witnesses through whom
lived reality is construed differently is often given as a characteristic assurance, but on many other occasions this same Character is rather a decon-
structive force who moves against every settlement, every certitude, and
every assurance. Or as Jürgen Moltmann has said of more belated, Christian claims for faith, the God given on the lips of witnesses is both "foundation" and "criticism," both the *power for life* who is profoundly generative
and authorizing as well as summoning and dispatching, but who is also a
critical principle standing as a check upon what these witnesses may say
against this Character.[32] Or more summarily, this testimony to God is a
claim that at the core of lived reality there is a mystery invested with transformative energy and with durable purposiveness. The witnessing community endlessly relearns, however, that embrace of that transformative energy
and durable purposiveness does nothing to minimize the inscrutable Otherness of the Character who inhabits such mystery.

The role of Old Testament theology as attendance upon the testimony
concerning this Character varies as we consider the various publics
addressed by such study. We may be guided by David Tracy's identification
of three publics that concern us—the academic, the ecclesial, and the
civic.[33] Of any work in Old Testament studies, it may be especially Old Testament theology that reaches beyond the limits of the discipline of Old Testament study itself to address those other publics.

1. Old Testament theology in the context of Old Testament studies, that
is, *within the academic community:*[34] There is no doubt that Old Testament
theology is related to and much informed by many different kinds of critical study, literary and historical.[35] It no longer pertains, moreover, that
these several modes of critical study are conducted in the service of theology, as might have been the case when theology could claim to be "queen of
the sciences." In a postmodern setting, it is clear that much of critical study
is taken as an end in itself, without any reference to theological issues, or in

some quarters critical study is undertaken precisely to defeat theological interpretation and eliminate the questions it purports to address.

Old Testament theology, in our present context of scholarship, has no leverage or need to be taken seriously by the guild of scholarship and has no mandate to insist upon its own claims. Nonetheless, we who take up the work of theological interpretation sense that critical study that is singularly preoccupied with historical or literary questions, or proceeds according to positivistic rationality that in principle nullifies Israel's testimony to God, in fact has failed to pay attention to the text or to the claims that are expressed and that invite the hearer's engagement. In the end, it seems clear that the Old Testament text is preoccupied not with historical questions nor even with literary finesse, though both literary and historical issues are fully present, but with the strange, sometimes violent, sometimes hidden, often unwelcome ways of this Holy Agent in the midst of life.

Much of historical and literary study, taken in and of itself, while perfectly legitimate, is conducted in a way that is "tone deaf" to the voice of the text. Thus Old Testament theology, if it is not reductive or coercive, may be an invitation that could keep the academic discipline from being turned in upon itself, preoccupied with greater and greater intensity on issues that matter less and less. In the end, the history of ancient Israel that can be recovered by positivistic categories does not seem to go anywhere that would interest the witnesses themselves, for when the Holy Character is deleted from the calculus of meaning, not much that matters remains.[36] In the same way, attentiveness to literary and rhetorical elements of the text seems to be the artistry of the sort of folk who are always pointing beyond the artistry itself to the artistry's true Subject, who defies critical decoding. It seems inevitable that the core claim of Old Testament theology—witness to the Character—will continue to live in discomfort with a kind of positivistic criticism that resists its very subject. Nonetheless, its work is to keep before the more general discipline the central Character without whom much of the rest of our study ends up being trivial.

2. Old Testament theology in the context of faith communities, that is, *ecclesial communities:*[37] Because Old Testament theology is here defined as speech about God, it is inevitable that reference will be made to those communities that intentionally engage in and attend to serious speech about God. There is an unresolvable tension between academic study and ecclesial study, if the former is defined in positivistic categories. But to define academic study in positivistic categories is itself an advocacy of special pleading and is not a necessary assumption. How the interplay of academic and ecclesial references is adjudicated seems largely to depend upon the interpreter, but to begin with an assumption of total separation is a premise that is not readily persuasive.[38]

But the more important ecclesial question concerns the tension and interplay between faith communities, Jewish and Christian, both of which look to these texts as Scripture.[39] It is now completely clear, especially through the work of Jon Levenson, that Old Testament theology historically has been an unashamedly Christian enterprise, or even more specifically, a Protestant enterprise. Such study, moreover, has been deeply marked by unthinking anti-Jewish interpretation, an outcome that is inescapable as long as work is done in isolation.

Moreover, Brevard Childs has made a powerful case that Jews and Christians read different Bibles, so that the theological interpretation among Christians and among Jews is different from the ground up.[40] This same view is reiterated from the Jewish side by Jon Levenson.[41] While the argument has much to commend it, it is not one by which I am persuaded. It is my judgment, rather, that theological interpretation of these Scriptures can and is better done by Jews and Christians together, who may part company in their reading only late, if at all. The ground for common reading is partly moral and historical, that Christian supersessionism and its consequent brutality require an alternative approach.[42] Beyond that and more important, however, is the generative, evocative character of the text and the Character dominant within it. It is evident that the Old Testament imagines toward the New, but it manifestly does not imagine exclusively toward the New. It is evident that Hebrew Scriptures imagine toward the Talmud, but they do not imagine exclusively toward the Talmud.[43]

Rather the Old Testament/Hebrew Scriptures imagine vigorously in pronouncedly polyvalent ways, an offer addressed to and received by both Jewish and Christian faith communities as authoritative for a life faith. But because the imaginative thrust of the text is richly generative beyond every interpretive domestication, it will not do for a subsequent faith community to construe itself as the exclusive receiver of that generativity. Thus it seems to me that it is not a mistake to see this text toward the New Testament, but it is a deep, substantive mistake to see this text *exclusively* toward the New Testament (and mistaken in a similar way to see it only toward the synagogue).[44]

The truth is that the ecclesial communities are summoned precisely to host this Character marked, on the lips of the witnesses, by inscrutable mystery, assertive will and energy, and inviolable purpose. And while that mystery, will, energy, and purpose may be provisionally linked to the Jewish community (in the claims of election and covenant) or to the Christian community (in the claims of Christology), the linkages are indeed provisional and contingent. As Old Testament theology may have as its work to summon academic scholarship away from trivialization and preoccupation with marginal matters, so Old Testament theology may summon ecclesial communities from certitudes that are excessive and exclusions that are idolatrous, by witnessing to the elusive but insistent reality of this Holy Character.

3. Old Testament theology *in public discourse:* If Old Testament theology is *a practice of reimagining lived reality with reference to this odd core*

Character, then Old Testament theology, in its furthest stretch, may speak past academic and ecclesial communities to be concerned with public discourse. I do not imagine that Old Testament theology can contribute specifically and concretely to questions of public policy and public morality, as interfaces between old text and public issues are exceedingly complicated.

But if the emerging dominant construal of reality in the global economy is the unfettered pursuit of private power by the manipulation of the "money government," then Old Testament theology as a witness to this Holy Character can indeed provide materials for an alternative imagination.[45] It seems evident that the more recent construal of the world in terms of privatized global economy is not one that will enhance our common life. Such a concept of the world, so it appears, ends either in self-sufficiency or in despair. In either case it offers a huge potential for brutality, either to fend off in active ways those who impinge and threaten, or simply by neglect to allow the disappearance of the noncompetitive.

It may be that from some other source can come an alternative to this dominant construal of reality, perhaps from what Robert Bellah terms the "republican" tradition.[46] It can hardly be doubted that some alternative construal of social reality is urgent among us. And if we work from the ground up, it is entirely plausible that *lived reality reimagined out from this Character who lives on the lips of these witnesses* could offer such a wholesale and compelling alternative.

IV

There is no doubt that Old Testament theology, in conversation with any of these three publics, proceeds with something of a "naïve realism," prepared to take the utterance of the witnessing text as a serious offer.[47] Such naïveté may be only provisional and instrumental, as the interpreter withholds a serious personal commitment, or that "naïve realism" may reflect (as in my case) the primal inclination of the practitioner. Either way, so it seems to me, the practitioner of Old Testament theology must move between a credulous fideism and a knowing, suspicious skepticism, wherein the former does not pay sufficient attention to the *problematic* of the witness, and the latter is *tone deaf* to the core claim of the witnesses.

At the moment and perhaps for the foreseeable future, Old Testament theology must work its way between two determined challenges. On the one hand, there are those whom I would term "*children of innocence,*" who are excessively credulous and who do not remain long with the elusive quality of the text, but immediately push the testimony along to the more reified claims of the ecclesial community, for example, in Christian parlance, to reduce the testimony into doctrinal categories. It appears to me that such innocence is much powered by *anxiety* that old truths are in jeopardy and the world does hold. The reduction of the testimony turns out to be a strategy for the recovery of a "lost coherence."

On the other hand, there are those whom I would term "*children of coercion*" who are exceedingly skeptical, but who do not linger long enough with the playful disjunctive quality of the Character, but immediately push the testimony to reified formulation which they then immediately are obligated to combat. It appears to me that such skepticism is rooted in *great rage,* not really rage at the text or even its claims, but rage rooted in old, hidden histories of coerciveness whose wounds remaining endlessly painful.

Both such *anxiety-rooted-in-innocence* and such *rage-rooted-in-coercion* are serious, endlessly powerful postures that are not easily overcome. It seems equally clear, however, that neither *anxiety* over a world that is passing or *rage* about a world that has injured is an adequate place from which to engage the Character who lives on the lips of the witnesses.

In a postmodern context where hegemonic claims of any sort are doubtful, Old Testament theology must play a modest role, not claim too much for itself, but stand in some interpretive continuity with ancient witnesses who imagined and uttered with radical difference. While embracing an appropriate modesty, however, Old Testament theology must have its own say, voice its own offer that claims no privilege but is not to be confused with any other claim. It could be, if done with authority but without any streak of arrogance, that Old Testament theology could invite:

- the academic community away from self-preoccupied triviality that is such a waste,
- the ecclesial communities away from excessive certitude that is idolatry, and
- the civic community away from brutality rooted in autonomy long enough to engage this summoning Mystery.

Anxiety and rage are real and legitimate. It remains to see if reading through them and past them is possible. The offer of these witnesses is sometimes as definite as "a God so near and a Torah so just" (Deut. 4:7-8). Sometimes the witness is as open and inviting as a question: "Where shall wisdom be found?" (Job 28:12). Either way, the witnesses invite beyond anxiety and beyond rage to a mystery whose name we know provisionally.

Abbreviations

AB	Anchor Bible
ABD	*Anchor Bible Dictionary*
BK	Biblischer Kommentor
BZAW	Beihefte zur *ZAW*
CBQ	*Catholic Biblical Quarterly*
ConBOT	Coniectanea biblica, Old Testament
Interp	*Interpretation*
JBL	*Journal of Biblical Literature*
JR	*Journal of Religion*
JSOT	*Journal for the Study of the Old Testament*
JSOTSup	Journal of the Study of the Old Testament—Supplement Series
OBT	Overtures to Biblical Theology
OTL	Old Testament Library
SBL	Society of Biblical Literature
SBLMS	SBL Monograph Series
SBT	Studies in Biblical Theology
SJT	*Scottish Journal of Theology*
VTS	Vetus Testamentum Supplements
WMANT	Wissenschaftliche Monographien zum Alten und Neuen Testament
ZAW	*Zeitschrift für die alttestamentliche Wissenschaft*
ZThK	*Zeitschrift für Theologie und Kirche*

Notes

1. Preaching as Sub-Version

1. Michael J. Buckley, *At the Origins of Modern Atheism* (New Haven: Yale Univ. Press, 1990).

2. For a review of the origins of these intellectual developments, see Paul Hazard, *The European Mind, 1680–1715: The Critical Years* (New York: Fordham Univ. Press, 1990). On the contemporary culmination in "Sheilaism," see Robert N. Bellah et al., *Habits of the Heart: Individualism and Commitment in American Life* (Berkeley: Univ. of California Press, 1985) 221, 235.

3. On the "complete unfamiliarity" of the Bible, see the classic statements of Karl Barth, "The Strange New World within the Bible," in *The Word of God and the Word of Man,* trans. D. Horton (New York: Harper and Brothers, 1957) 28–50; and Martin Buber, "The Man of Today and the Jewish Bible," in *On the Bible: Eighteen Studies,* ed. Nahum N. Glatzer (New York: Schocken, 1968) 1–13. On the *Jewish* "unfamiliarity" of the text, see Susan A. Handelman, *The Slayers of Moses: The Emergence of Rabbinic Interpretation in Modern Literary Theory* (Albany: SUNY Press, 1982).

4. On the relation of *how* and *who* in the text, see Gail R. O'Day, *The Word Disclosed: John's Story and Narrative Preaching* (St. Louis: CBP, 1987).

5. On the relation between Jewish modes of interpretation and Freud, see *Midrash and Literature,* ed. Susan A. Handelman, Gail R. O'Day, Geoffrey H. Hartman, and Sanford Budick (New Haven: Yale Univ. Press, 1986); and John Murray Cuddihy, *The Ordeal of Civility: Freud, Marx, Lévi-Strauss and the Jewish Struggle with Modernity* (New York: Basic Books, 1974).

6. On violence in the character of God, see Renita J. Weems, *Battered Love: Marriage, Sex, and Violence in the Hebrew Prophets* (OBT; Minneapolis: Fortress Press, 1995); and Regina M. Schwartz, *The Curse of Cain: The Violent Legacy of Monotheism* (Chicago: Univ. of Chicago Press, 1997).

7. On the power of the myth of scarcity, see the theological critique of M. Douglas Meeks, *God the Economist: The Doctrine of God and Political Economy* (Minneapolis: Fortress Press, 1989), and the hermeneutical analysis of Schwartz, *Curse of Cain.*

8. Fox Butterfield, *All God's Children: The Bosket Family and the American Tradition of Violence* (New York: Knopf, 1995).

9. On the psalms of complaint and lament, see the comprehensive study of Patrick D. Miller, *They Cried to the Lord: The Form and Theology of Biblical Prayer* (Minneapolis: Fortress Press, 1994).

10. On such practices as "signals of oddity" in the Jewish community, see Jacob Neusner, *The Enchantments of Judaism: Rites of Transformation from Birth through Death* (New York: Basic Books, 1987).

11. Walter Brueggemann, *Cadences of Home: Preaching Among Exiles* (Louisville: Westminster John Knox, 1997). See also Frederick Buechner, *The Longing for Home: Recollections and Reflections* (San Francisco: HarperSanFrancisco, 1996).

2. Life-or-Death, De-Privileged Communication

1. On the production of atheism as a viable alternative in modernism, see Michael J. Buckley, *At the Origins of Modern Atheism* (New Haven: Yale Univ. Press, 1987).

2. I have explicated this theme at length in Walter Brueggemann, *Theology of the Old Testament: Testimony, Dispute, Advocacy* (Minneapolis: Fortress Press, 1997).

3. Hayden White, *The Content of the Form: Narrative Discourse and Historical Representation* (Baltimore: Johns Hopkins Univ. Press, 1987) 20, comments on the work of a historian and the construction of a historical account:

> It is the fact that they can be recorded otherwise, in an order of narrative, that makes them, at one and the same time, questionable as to their authenticity and susceptible to being considered as tokens of reality. In order to qualify as historical, an event must be susceptible to at least two narrations of its occurrence. Unless at least two versions of the same set of events can be imagined, there is no reason for the historian to take upon himself the authority of giving the true account of what really happened.

Mutatis mutandis, the same is true for the preacher. The only reason the preaching task is important is that the same data of life can be construed differently, that is, without reference to Yahweh who is the main character in "our" version. This recognition that the truth of the matter can be given in an alternative, credible version is an important facet of our new preaching situation.

4. This is in general the burden of the writing program of Elie Wiesel. Reference may be made, for example, to Wiesel, *The Trial of God* (New York: Random House, 1978). An assessment of this work concerning testimony by Wiesel is offered by Robert McAfee Brown, *Elie Wiesel: Messenger to All Humanity* (Notre Dame: Univ. of Notre Dame Press, 1983); and see Wiesel's own account of his work, *Memoirs: All Rivers Run to the Sea* (New York:

Knopf, 1995). The most poignant statement of Wiesel on the theme of "testimony" is Wiesel, "The Holocaust as Literary Inspiration," in *Dimensions of Holocaust* (Evanston: Northwestern Univ. Press, 1977) 9: "If the Greeks invented tragedy, the Romans the epistle, and the Renaissance the sonnet, our generation invented a new literature, that of testimony." Wiesel refers to the requirement of testimony with reference to the Holocaust, because the truth of the Holocaust is *in dispute* and the outcome depends upon the *witnesses*.

5. Arthur W. Frank, *The Wounded Storyteller: Body, Illness, and Ethics* (Chicago: Univ. of Chicago Press, 1995).

6. The same qualities mark the primal stories that the early church told about Jesus that became the basis for the worship and faith of the early church.

7. I will stick to the Old Testament, but it is clear that the same deprivileged situation operates in the New Testament, as is evident in Paul's testimony before imperial officials in the book of Acts.

8. It is on this basis that scholars characteristically declare that the rise of monotheism in the Old Testament is linked to 2 Isaiah. See the evidence summarized by Bernhard Lang, *Monotheism and the Prophetic Minority: An Essay in Biblical History and Sociology* (The Social World of Biblical Antiquity Series 1; Sheffield: Almond Press, 1983); and more recently, *The Triumph of Elohim: From Yahwisms to Judaisms,* ed. Diana Vikander Edelman (Grand Rapids: Eerdmans, 1995). However that may be, it is unmistakable that the establishment of monotheism was no concern of the poet.

9. The "education" of Pharaoh through the processes of the exodus narrative is a case in point. At the outset, Pharaoh disclaims any awareness of Yahweh (Exod. 5:2). By 8:25 he acknowledges "your God." In 8:28 he again refers to "your God," and asks for prayers. In 10:16 he confesses sin against "your God" and by 12:32 recognizes that blessing is in the power of the God of Moses. The learning curve for Pharaoh is perhaps typical for those who live out of a different, hegemonic narrative.

10. *New York Times* (June 11, 1997).

3. Together in the Spirit — Beyond Seductive Quarrels

This address was presented, by student invitation, at Candler School of Theology, April 16, 1997.

1. See Karl Barth, *Church Dogmatics* vol. 3/3, trans. G. W. Bromiley (Edinburgh: T. & T. Clark, 1960) 289–368; Jon D. Levenson, *Creation and the Persistence of Evil: The Jewish Drama of Divine Omnipotence* (San Francisco: Harper and Row, 1988); and Fredrik Lindström, *Suffering and Sin: Interpretations of Illness in the Individual Complaint Psalms* (ConBOT 37; Stockholm: Almqvist & Wiksell, 1994).

2. See David R. Blumenthal, *Facing the Abusing God: A Theology of Protest* (Louisville: Westminster John Knox, 1993).

3. See Philip Haille, *Lest Innocent Blood Be Shed* (San Francisco: Harper-Collins, 1994).

4. See Jack B. Rogers and Donald K. McKim, *The Authority and Interpretation of the Bible: An Historical Approach* (San Francisco: Harper and Row, 1979).

5. See Walter Brueggemann, *Cadences of Home: Preaching Among Exiles* (Louisville: Westminster John Knox, 1997).

6. On the theological use of the term *gospel* (*baśar*), see Walter Brueggemann, *Biblical Perspectives on Evangelism: Living in a Three-Storied Universe* (Nashville: Abingdon, 1993) 26–30.

7. Taylor Branch, *Parting the Waters: America in the King Years, 1954–1963* (New York: Simon & Schuster, 1988) 162.

4. Reading as Wounded and as Haunted

1. On the religious prehistory of the canon, see Rainer Albertz, *A History of Israelite Religion in the Old Testament Period* 2 vols., trans. J. Bowden (OTL; Louisville: Westminster John Knox, 1994).

2. James A. Sanders, *Torah and Canon* (Philadelphia: Fortress Press, 1972).

3. Peter L. Berger and Thomas Luckmann, *The Social Construction of Reality: A Treatise in the Sociology of Knowledge* (Garden City, N.Y.: Doubleday, 1966).

4. On the double-theodicy characteristic of communities, see Peter L. Berger, *The Sacred Canopy: Elements of a Sociological Theory of Religion* (Garden City, N.Y.: Doubleday, 1967) 53–80.

5. The phrase "contrast society" is prominent in the work of Norbert Lohfink.

6. Hans-Joachim Kraus, *Die prophetische Verkundigung des Rechts in Israel* (Zollikon: Evangelischer Verlag, 1957).

7. Gerhard von Rad, *Studies in Deuteronomy*, trans. D. Stalker (SBT 1/9; Chicago: Henry Regnery, 1953). See also Martin Noth, "The 'Representation' of the O.T. in Proclamation," in *Essays on Old Testament Hermeneutics*, ed. Claus Westermann, trans. J. L. Mays (Richmond: John Knox, 1963) 76–88.

8. Gerald T. Sheppard, *Wisdom as a Hermeneutical Construct* (BZAW 151; Berlin: de Gruyter, 1980). See also John Barton, *The Oracles of God: Perceptions of Ancient Prophecy in Israel after the Exile* (Oxford: Oxford Univ. Press, 1986).

9. Charles Altieri, *Canons and Consequences: Reflections on the Ethical Force of Imaginative Ideals* (Evanston: Northwestern Univ. Press, 1990) 22.

10. Ibid., 23–25.

11. Ibid., 33.

12. Ibid., 34.

13. Ibid.

14. Ibid., 36.

15. Regina M. Schwartz, *The Curse of Cain: The Violent Legacy of Monotheism* (Chicago: Univ. of Chicago Press, 1997) 146.

16. Ibid., 147.

17. Ibid., 119.

18. Programmatically, the Jesus Seminar is an act of suspicion, for it means to expose the claims of canon as unreliable concerning the character of Jesus.

19. Paul Ricoeur, *Freud and Philosophy: An Essay on Interpretation*, trans. D. Savage (New Haven: Yale Univ. Press, 1970) 33.

20. Ibid., 34.

21. John Murray Cuddihy, *The Ordeal of Civility: Freud, Marx, Levi-Straus and the Jewish Struggle with Modernity* (New York: Basic Books, 1974).

22. On Ricoeur's program, see Mark I. Wallace, *The Second Naiveté: Barth, Ricoeur, and the New Yale School* (Studies in American Biblical Hermeneutics 6; Macon: Mercer Univ. Press, 1990).

23. See Walter Brueggemann, *The Message of the Psalms: A Theological Commentary* (Minneapolis: Augsburg, 1984).

24. David Tracy, *The Analogical Imagination: Christian Theology and the Culture of Pluralism* (New York: Crossroad, 1981) 119–20.

25. Michael J. Buckley, *At the Origins of Modern Atheism* (New Haven: Yale Univ. Press, 1987) 336.

26. Ibid., 337–38.

27. Ibid., 359.

28. Ibid., 362.

29. See the same options in the term by Ellen F. Davis, "'And Pharaoh Will Change His Mind . . .' (Ezek. 32:13)" (unpublished SBL paper, Washington, D.C., November 20, 1993).

30. Jürgen Moltmann, *The Crucified God: The Cross of Christ as the Foundation and the Criticism of Christian Theology* (New York: Harper and Row, 1974) 243.

31. On the "theology of glory," see Douglas John Hall, *Lighten Our Darkness: Toward an Indigenous Theology of the Cross* (Philadelphia: Westminster, 1976).

32. Emil L. Fackenheim, *To Mend the World: Foundations of Post-Holocaust Thought* (New York: Schocken, 1989) 11.

33. Claus Westermann, "The Role of the Lament in the Theology of the Old Testament," *Interp* 28 (1974) 30. On the dialectic of protest and submissiveness, see Jon D. Levenson, *Creation and the Persistence of Evil: The Jewish Drama of Divine Omnipotence* (San Francisco: Harper and Row, 1988) 140–48 and *passim*.

34. See David R. Blumenthal, *Facing the Abusing God: A Theology of Protest* (Louisville: Westminster John Knox, 1993).

35. Westermann, "The Role of Lament," 33–34. On the relation between sin and suffering, see Fredrik Lindström, *Suffering and Sin: Interpretations of Illness in the Individual Complaint Psalms* (ConBOT 37; Stockholm: Almqvist & Wiksell, 1994).

5. Four Indispensable Conversations among Exiles

This address was presented as a lecture in the Lee Institute, Ladue Chapel, St. Louis, Missouri, October 21, 1996.

1. Frederick Buechner, *Longing for Home: Recollections and Reflections* (San Francisco: HarperSanFrancisco, 1996) 110.

2. Ibid., 128.

3. Ibid., 140.

4. Will Lamartine Thompson (1847–1909), "Softly and Tenderly," first published 1880.

7. Texts That Linger, Not Yet Overcome

1. I regard this as especially a problem for Christians and will so discuss the matter. This is partly because there is an inherent propensity in Christianity to give closure to its thought, and partly because of the long history of Christianity as a dominant cultural power. It is not, however, a peculiarly Christian problem. Thus, for example, see Jon D. Levenson, *Creation and the Persistence of Evil: The Jewish Drama of Divine Omnipotence* (San Francisco: Harper & Row, 1988) 3, and his reference to Yehezkel Kaufmann, who exhibits something like the same propensity to closure.

2. On this aspect of Crenshaw's work, see Walter Brueggemann, "James L. Crenshaw: Faith Lingering at the Edges," *Religious Studies Review* 20.2 (April, 1994) 103–10. See Crenshaw's comments in the same issue, which agree with this assessment.

3. In this volume the term set out as the topic by the editors is "darkness," which serves as a cover term for all of these negativities. I am not unaware that such a usage flirts with offensiveness for African Americans, and use the term only because the editors have focused us on that term. I trust colleagues will recognize both the problem of that usage and its intention in these essays.

4. This problem has received much more attention from Jewish thinkers than from Christian thinkers, no doubt because of the Christian eagerness to give closure, as acknowledged in n. 1. Thus, for example, we may refer to Martin Buber's "Eclipse," Andre Neher's "exile" and "silence," and the several articulations of Emil Fackenheim.

5. There is of course a vast literature on Psalm 22. Among the more recent and most helpful are Ellen F. Davis, "Exploding the Limits: Form and Function in Psalm 22," *JSOT* 53 (1992) 93–105, and John S. Kselman, "'Why Have You Abandoned Me?' A Rhetorical Study of Psalm 22," in *Art and Meaning: Rhetoric in Biblical Literature*, ed. David J. A. Clines et al. (JSOTSup 19; Sheffield: JSOT Press, 1982) 172–98.

6. By the phrase "experience and expression," I refer to Paul Ricoeur, "Biblical Hermeneutics," *Semeia* 4 (1975) 107–45, and his notions of "limit experience" and "limit expression." These texts of "darkness" are "limit expressions" that give Israel access to its "limit experiences."

7. Jürgen Moltmann, *The Crucified God: The Cross of Christ as the Foundation and Criticism of Christian Theology* (Minneapolis: Fortress Press, 1993) 146–51, 207, 218, and passim.

8. On the cross of Jesus as an enactment of the "darkness," see the powerful statement of Douglas John Hall, *Toward an Indigenous Theology of the Cross* (Philadelphia: Westminster Press, 1976). Moltmann, *The Crucified God*, 243, has the very nice phrase for the significance of the cross: "The Fatherlessness of the Son is matched by the Sonlessness of the Father . . ."

9. On grief over the destruction of Jerusalem as paradigmatic grief for Jews, see Alan Mintz, *Hurban: Responses to Catastrophe in Hebrew Literature* (New York: Columbia University Press, 1984). See especially his programmatic statement on p. 2.

10. This sense of God's absence is very different from the conventional Deuteronomic notion that God's absence is a result of Israel's sin. On the tension Lamentations has with both Deuteronomic and Zion traditions, see the discussion of Bertil Albrektson, *Studies in the Text and Theology of the Book of Lamentations* (Studia Theologica Lundensia 21; Lund: Gleerup, 1963).

11. On complaint and petition, see Erhard S. Gerstenberger *Der bittende Mensch* (WMANT 51; Neukirchen-Vluyn: Neukirchener, 1980).

12. The translation is that of Delbert R. Hillers, *Lamentations: A New Translation with Introduction and Commentary* (AB 7A; Garden City, N.Y.: Doubleday, 1972) 96. See his comments on pp. 100–101.

13. See Mintz, *Hurban* 41–46, on the relation of Lamentations and Second Isaiah. My former student, Tod Linafelt, has begun important work on this connection.

14. On this text, see Walter Brueggemann "A Shattered Transcendence? Exile and Restoration," in *Biblical Theology: Problems and Prospects*, ed. Steven J. Kraftchick, et al. (Nashville: Abingdon, 1995).

15. Mintz, *Hurban* 23–25, suggests that the use of the image of a raped, dying woman rather than a dead woman is used in order that the suffering, pain, and grief may be ongoing and not yet (or ever) terminated: "The raped and defiled woman who survives . . . is a living witness to a pain that knows no release."

16. On our "usual theological readings" which render texts "unreadable," see Susan A. Handelman, *The Slayers of Moses: The Emergence of Rabbinic Interpretation in Modern Literary Theory* (Albany: SUNY Press, 1982). Handelman's study of course informs much of the argument of my paper.

17. This is, for example, the affirmation of the hymn "Holy, Holy, Holy" by Reginald Heber:

> Holy, holy, holy! though the darkness hide thee,
> though the eye of sinful man thy glory many not see . . .

On that assumption, God is not absent, but only unseen because of sin.

18. On such a "tight moral structure," see Klaus Koch, "Gibt es ein Vergeltungsdogma im Alten Testament?" *ZThK* 52 (1955) 1–42, and an abridged English translation, "Is There a Doctrine of Retribution in the Old Testament?" in *Theodicy in the Old Testament* ed. James L. Crenshaw (Issues in Religion and Theology 4; Philadelphia: Fortress Press, 1983) 57–87, and the more nuanced discussion of Patrick D. Miller Jr., *Sin and Judgment in the Prophets: A Stylistic and Theological Analysis* (Chico, Calif. : Scholars Press, 1982).

19. This is from time to time the strategy of John Calvin. On these verses, Calvin, *Commentary on the Book of the Prophet Isaiah,* trans. William Pringle (Calvin's Commentaries 8; Grand Rapids: Baker, 1979) 140, writes:

> When he says that he forsook his people, it is a sort of admission of the fact. We are adopted by God in such a manner that we cannot be rejected by him on account of the treachery of men; for he is faithful, so that he will not cast off or abandon his people. What the Prophet says in this passage must therefore refer to our feelings and to outward appearance, because we seem to be rejected by God when we do not perceive his presence and protection. And it is necessary that we should thus feel God's wrath . . . But we must also perceive his mercy; and because it is infinite and eternal, we shall find that all afflictions in comparison of it are light and momentary.

20. This is the perspective of Brevard S. Childs, *Biblical Theology of the Old and New Testaments: Theological Reflection on the Christian Bible* (Minneapolis: Fortress Press, 1992).

21. The whole matter of a "canonical reading" is not obvious in its meaning. Childs himself has over time suggested a variety of different dimensions to the notion of "canonical" and so far as I am aware only in his most recent book, *Biblical Theology*, has he concluded that "canonical" means according to a theological "rule of faith."

22. I am grateful to my colleague, Shirley Guthrie, for clarifying this point for me. He and I have had fruitful exchanges about this matter. In the

end, I suspect we do not agree. Nonetheless I have come to understand better because of his instruction, and am able to rethink matters in ways reflective of his persuasive and gentle influence.

23. For a recent critical assessment of Wellhausen, see *Julius Wellhausen and His Prolegomena to the History of Israel*, ed. Douglas A. Knight *Semeia* 25 (1983). On the world of Darwin and the tensions between nineteenth-century science and conventional religion, see Adrian Desmond and James Moore, *Darwin* (New York: Warner Books, 1991).

24. For a dramatic understanding of Yahweh that moves in a postcritical direction, see Dale Patrick, *The Rendering of God in the Old Testament* (OBT; Philadelphia: Fortress Press, 1981).

25. It is my impression that in his most recent work, *Biblical Theology*, Brevard S. Childs attends to the problem of referentiality in a way that results in a God "out there."

26. On a dramatic mode of theological interpretation, see in addition to Patrick the work of Hans Frei and Walter Brueggemann, *Texts Under Negotiation: The Bible and Postmodern Imagination* (Minneapolis: Fortress Press, 1993). Most broadly, see Hans Urs von Balthasar, *Theo-Drama: Theological Dramatic Theory I, Prolegomena* (San Francisco: Ignatius Press, 1988), *II The Dramatis Personae: Man in God* (San Francisco: Ignatius, 1990).

27. Brevard S. Childs, "The Sensus Literalis of Scripture: An Ancient and Modern Problem," in *Beiträge zur Alttestamentlichen Theologie: Festschrift für Wälther Zimmerli zum 70. Geburtstag*, ed. Herbert Donner et al. (Göttingen: Vandenhoeck & Ruprecht, 1977) 80–93, has offered a most provocative understanding of "literal sense." Childs, of course, knows that his view is not without problem and is not uncontested.

28. Richard A. Lanham, *The Motives of Eloquence: Literary Rhetoric in the Renaissance* (New Haven: Yale Univ. Press, 1976).

29. Ibid., 1.

30. Ibid., 4.

31. Stanley Fish, "Rhetoric," in *Critical Terms for Literary Study*, ed. Frank Lentricchia and Thomas McLaughlin (Chicago: University of Chicago Press, 1990) 215.

32. For a recent reconsideration of the Sophists, see Susan C. Jarratt, *Rereading the Sophists: Classical Rhetoric Refigured* (Carbondale: Southern Illinois Univ. Press, 1991). I am grateful to Perky Daniel for this reference and for suggesting this line of reflection to me.

33. Richard Rorty, *Consequences of Pragmatism* (Minneapolis: Univ. of Minnesota Press, 1982) 92, quoted by Fish, "Rhetoric," 221.34. Fish, "Rhetoric," 222.

35. James L. Crenshaw, "Wisdom and Authority: Sapiential Rhetoric and Its Warrants," in *Congress Volume: Vienna, 1980,* ed. J. A. Emerton (VTS 32; Leiden: Brill, 1981) 10-29. On the constitutive power of speech,

see Walter Brueggemann, *Israel's Praise: Doxology against Idolatry and Ideology* (Philadelphia: Fortress Press, 1988) 1–53.

36. Brevard S. Childs, *Biblical Theology in Crisis* (Philadelphia: Westminster, 1970); *The Book of Exodus: A Critical, Theological Commentary* (OTL; Philadelphia: Westminster, 1974); *Old Testament Theology in a Canonical Context* (Philadelphia: Fortress Press, 1985); and *Biblical Theology.*

37. *Biblical Theology*, 20, 67, 724, passim.

38. Ibid., 20. On the problem of "reference" with particular attention to Hans Frei, see Frei, *The Eclipse of Biblical Narrative: A Study in Eighteenth and Nineteenth Century Hermeneutics* (New Haven: Yale University Press, 1974), and "The 'Literal Reading' of Biblical Narrative in the Christian Tradition: Does It Stretch or Will It Break?" in *The Bible and the Narrative Tradition*, ed. Frank McConnell (New York: Oxford Univ. Press, 1986) 36–77. On Frei's work vis-à-vis Childs, see Gerald T. Sheppard, *The Future of the Bible: Beyond Liberalism and Literalism* (Toronto: United Church Publishing House, 1990) 41–42, and Charles Lamar Campbell, *Preaching Jesus: Hans Frei's Theology and the Contours of a Postliberal Homiletic* (doctoral dissertation, Duke Univ., 1993).

39. Childs, *Biblical Theology* 665.

40. Ibid., 80.

41. Ibid., 83.

42. Ibid., 86.

43. David R. Blumenthal, *Facing the Abusing God: A Theology of Protest* (Louisville: Westminster John Knox, 1993).

44. Ibid., 47–48.

45. Ibid., 9.

46. Ibid., 239.

47. Ibid.

48. Ibid., 247, 248.

49. Ibid., 239.

50. Childs, *Biblical Theology* 335.

51. Ibid., 335–36.

52. See Patrick, *The Rendering of God*, 28–60.

53. See the comment of Robert Alter, *The World of Biblical Literature* (New York: Basic Books, 1992) 133, on "excavative" reading.

54. David Tracy, *The Analogical Imagination: Christian Theology and the Culture of Pluralism* (New York: Crossroad, 1981) has explored a notion of "classic" as a category for religious texts.

55. The term "second naïveté" is Ricoeur's. See Mark I. Wallace, *The Second Naiveté: Barth, Ricoeur, and the New Yale Theology* (Studies in American Biblical Hermeneutics 6; Macon, Ga.: Mercer Univ. Press, 1990).

8. Crisis-Evoked, Crisis, Resolving Speech

1. On the conceptual as "second level" theological discourse, see Paul Ricoeur, in many places, for example, *The Philosophy of Paul Ricoeur*, ed. Charles E. Reagan and David Stewart (Boston: Beacon, 1978) 239–45.

2. Brevard S. Childs, *Biblical Theology of the Old and New Testaments: Theological Reflection on the Christian Bible* (Minneapolis: Fortress Press, 1993) is a recent, formidable example of a very quick move to conceptual discourse.

3. On such a depth of jeopardy, see Eric J. Cassell, *The Nature of Suffering and the Goals of Medicine* (New York: Oxford Univ. Press, 1991), who understands the threat against "intactness" to be the root of suffering, as distinct from pain. In these crises of ancient Israel, the intactness of Israel is under threat.

4. Paul Ricoeur, "Biblical Hermeneutics," *Semeia* 4 (1975) 108–45.

5. On the cruciality of genre study for biblical theology, see John J. Collins, "Is a Critical Biblical Theology Possible?" in *The Hebrew Bible and Its Interpreters*, ed. William Henry Propp et al. (Winona Lake, Ind.: Eisenbrauns, 1990) 1–17. I am in substantial agreement with Collins.

6. On chapters 32–34, see the interpretation by R. W. L. Moberly, *At the Mountain of God: Story and Theology in Exodus 32–34* (JSOTSup. 22; Sheffield: JSOT Press, 1983).

7. On the theological, ideological intent of these chapters, see Thomas B. Dozeman, *God on the Mountain: A Study of Redaction, Theology and Canon in Exodus 19–24* (SBLMS 37; Atlanta: Scholars Press, 1989), and more generally Norman K. Gottwald, *The Tribes of Yahweh: A Sociology of the Religion of Liberated Israel, 1250–1050 B.C.* (Maryknoll, N.Y.: Orbis, 1979) 100–114.

8. Among the most helpful of these discussions is Phyllis Trible, *God and the Rhetoric of Sexuality* (OBT; Philadelphia: Fortress Press, 1978) chapter 1.

9. The second, negative part of the divine oracle does indeed recur, as for example in Nahum 1:2-3, on which see J. J. M. Roberts, *Nahum, Habakkuk, and Zephaniah* (OTL; Louisville: Westminster John Knox, 1991) 49–50. In the majority of uses of this text, however, this part of the oracle is dropped.

10. It is not certain that the text is to be regarded as a unity, nor is it certain that the text refers in the first instant to the crisis of 721. The finished form of the text, however, permits us to assume an intended unity and makes most sense in light of that crisis. In their commentary, Francis I. Andersen and David Noel Freedman, *Hosea, a New Translation with Introduction and Commentary* (AB 24; Garden City, N.Y.: Doubleday, 1980) treat the text as a unity. On p. 263, they note links to Exod. 34:6, and on p. 264 comment on the two parts of the text in relation to each other.

11. David J. A. Clines, "Hosea 2: Structure and Interpretation," in *Studia Biblica 1978 I* (JSOTSup 11; Sheffield: JSOT Press, 1979) 83–103.

12. It is increasingly evident to scholars that the divorce and marriage metaphor functions as a powerful sexist metaphor that serves interests other than those intended by the poet. One cannot, however, disregard the metaphor in its intention. In interpretation, one must be aware of the unintended spin-off in our contemporary usage of the text.

13. John Barton has made the case well that there is not a complete "match" between historical event and literary expression. One must allow for playful, interpretive freedom in the prophets, whose words stand at an interpretive distance from the history upon which they reflect.

14. See Walter Brueggemann, "The Uninflected 'Therefore' of Hosea 4:1-3," in *Reading from This Place*, ed. Fernando F. Segovia and Mary Ann Tolbert (Minneapolis: Fortress Press, 1995) 231–49.

15. See the same triad in Hos. 4:3.

16. For example, Isa. 5:7; 9:7; 56:1; Amos 5:7, 24; 6:12.

17. The verb *ḥšq* in Deut. 7:7, 10:15 suggests the intense passion that may be assigned to Yahweh in relation to Israel.

18. Daniel S. Smith, *The Religion of the Landless: The Social Context of the Babylonian Exile* (Bloomington: Meyer-Stone, 1989) has shown how harsh the exile was. For more conventional treatments, see Peter R. Ackroyd, *Exile and Restoration: A Study of Hebrew Thought of the Sixth Century B.C.* (OTL; Philadelphia: Westminster Press, 1968); and Ralph W. Klein, *Israel in Exile: A Theological Interpretation* (OBT; Philadelphia: Fortress Press, 1979).

19. Alan Mintz, *Hurban: Responses to Catastrophe in Hebrew Literature* (New York: Columbia Univ. Press, 1984) provides the most poignant discussion of that trauma and the history of discourse that has been generated out of that crisis.

20. Mintz, *Hurban*, makes clear that it is speech that permits redemptive grief and at the same time precludes despair and resignation.

21. On this text, see Walter Brueggemann, "A Shattered Transcendence? Exile and Restoration," in *Biblical Theology: Problems and Prospects*, ed. Steven J. Kraftchick et al. (Nashville: Abingdon, 1995).

22. Mintz, *Hurban*, discerningly suggests that the poetry of Lamentations does not portray the city as a dead woman, but as an enduringly savaged, raped woman, because in that way the suffering is sustained and not completed, as it would be by death.

23. On the social situation of the widow in ancient Israel, see Paula S. Hiebert, "Whence Shall Help Come to Me? The Biblical Widow," in *Gender and Difference in Ancient Israel*, ed. Peggy L. Day (Minneapolis: Fortress Press, 1989) 125–41.

24. See my comments on "For a moment" in "A Shattered Transcendence."

25. On the social function of the redeemer, see A. R. Johnson, "The Primary Meaning of *g'l*," in *Congress Volume: Copenhagen 1953* (VTS 1; Leiden: Brill, 1953) 66–77, and Jeremiah Unterman, "Redemption, Old Testament," in *ABD* 5 (1992) 650–54.

26. On this text, see Walter Brueggemann, "This Is Like . . ." *Pulpit Digest* (May/June, 1991) 5–8.

27. On the use of such mythic-cosmic language in relation to historical experience, see Frank Moore Cross, *Canaanite Myth and Hebrew Epic: Essays in the History of the Religion of Israel* (Cambridge: Harvard Univ. Press, 1973) 77–144, and Thomas Mann, *Divine Presence and Guidance in Israelite Traditions: The Typology of Exaltation* (Baltimore: Johns Hopkins Univ. Press, 1977) 123–43.

28. For the Near Eastern placement of the phrase, see Bernard F. Batto, "The Covenant of Peace: A Neglected Ancient Near Eastern Motif," *CBQ* 49 (1987) 187–211.

29. Brevard S. Childs, *Biblical Theology*, 82–83 and passim, has a firm passion for the "reality of God" as it is given us in the text, and he refuses any hermeneutical distance between text and reality. It is unfortunate, however, that Childs is unwilling to follow the actual contours of the text for this "reality," but promptly moves from the textual contours to distanced conceptualization. I quite agree with Childs about the text links to "reality," but want to stay with the text much longer than does Childs.

30. On such an about face in the text, see Walter Brueggemann, "The 'Uncared For' Now Cared For (Jer. 30:12-17): A Methodological Consideration," *JBL* 104 (1985) 419–28.

31. It is, of course, problematic to say that Israel's situation "causes" Yahweh to reverse field. It is likely that the distinction between "cause" and "motivation" by Paul Ricoeur, "Explanation and Understanding," *From Text to Action: Essays in Hermeneutics II*, trans. Kathleen Blamey and John B. Thompson (Evanston: Northwestern Univ. Press, 1991) 125–43, will help in this difficulty. On an alternative "theory of action," see also Charles Taylor, *Human Agency and Language: Philosophical Papers 1* (Cambridge: Cambridge Univ. Press, 1985) 77–96 and passim.

32. See C. B. MacPherson, *The Political Theory of Possessive Individualism: Hobbes to Locke* (New York: Oxford Univ. Press, 1962).

33. Baruch A. Levine, *Numbers 1–20: A New Translation with Introduction and Commentary* (AB 4; New York: Doubleday, 1993) 33, comments, "God accedes to Moses' request in a uniquely dramatic statement, as if in obedience to Moses."

34. Translation is by Delbert R. Hillers, *Lamentations: A New Translation with Introduction and Commentary* (AB 7A; Garden City, N.Y.: Doubleday, 1972) 50.

35. Hans-Joachim Kraus, *Klagelieder (Threni)*, BK 20 (Neukirchen-Vluyn: Neukirchener, 1960) 62.

36. See John S. Kselman, "A Note on Psalm 85:9-10," *CBQ* 46 (1984) 23–27, on textual problems and more generally, the commentaries of Kraus and Weiser.

37. Hans-Joachim Kraus, *Psalms 60–150: A Commentary*, trans. H. C. Oswald (Minneapolis: Augsburg, 1989) 175.

38. The outcome for the reordered land is not unlike the abundance promised and anticipated in Hosea 2:21-22.

39. Artur Weiser, *The Psalms: A Commentary*, trans. H. Hartwell (OTL; Philadelphia: Westminster, 1962) 574.

40. Isak Dinesen, *Babette's Feast and Other Anecdotes of Destiny* (New York: Vintage, 1988) 6. See the shrewd use made of the tale by Lewis B. Smedes, *Shame and Grace: Healing the Shame We Don't Deserve* (San Francisco: Harper, 1993) 99–101.

41. *Babette's Feast*, 6.

42. Ibid., 7.

43. Ibid., 39–40.

44. Ibid., 42.

45. Ibid., 43.

9. The Role of Old Testament Theology in Old Testament Interpretation

1. It was Luther's intention to interpret the Bible and its gospel apart from the interpretive controls of the church. Thus biblical theology became an enterprise distinct from church theology. It is instructive that Hans-Joachim Kraus, *Geschichte der historisch-kiritischen Erforschung des Alten Testaments* (3rd ed.; Neukirchen-Vluyn: Neukirchener, 1982) 6–24, begins his study of biblical criticism with the rubric *"sola scriptura."*

2. See Henning Graf Reventlow, *The Authority of the Bible and the Rise of the Modern World,* trans. John Bowden (Philadelphia: Fortress Press, 1985).

3. Gabler's decisive lecture is available in its pertinent parts in English by John H. Sandys-Wunsch and Laurence Eldredge, "J. P. Gabler and the Distinction between Biblical and Dogmatic Theology: Translation, Commentary, and Discussion of His Originality," *SJT* 33 (1980) 133–58.

4. Ben C. Ollenburger, "Biblical Theology: Situating the Discipline," in *Understanding the Word: Essays in Honor of Bernhard W. Anderson,* ed. James T. Butler et al. (JSOTSup 37; Sheffield: JSOT Press, 1985) 37–62. See also Rolf P. Knierim, "On Gabler," in *The Task of Old Testament Theology: Substance, Method, and Cases* (Grand Rapids: Eerdmans, 1995) 495–556.

5. Julius Wellhausen, *Prolegomena to the History of Israel* (Edinburgh: Adam & Charles Black, 1885).

6. *Der Römerbrief* was offered in English as *The Epistle to the Romans,* trans. E. C. Hoskyns (London: Oxford Univ. Press, 1933).

7. The pivotal essay for von Rad, surely reflecting the confessional crisis of Barmen is "The Form-Critical Problem of the Hexateuch," in *The Prob-

lem of the Hexateuch and Other Essays, trans. E. W. T. Dicken (New York: McGraw-Hill, 1966) 1–78. The belated English translations of the more comprehensive works are Walter Eichrodt, *Theology of the Old Testament* 2 vols., trans. John Bowden (OTL; Philadelphia: Westminster, 1961, 1967); von Rad, *Old Testament Theology* 2 vols., trans. D. M. G. Stalker (New York: Harper, 1962, 1965).

8. G. Ernest Wright, *God Who Acts: Biblical Theology as Recital* (SBT 1/8; London: SCM, 1952). See also Wright, *The Old Testament against Its Environment* (SBT 1/2 London: SCM, 1950).

9. On the "Short Century," see Eric Hobsbawm, *The Age of Extremes: A History of the World 1914–1991* (New York: Pantheon, 1994). The "short century" refers to the time from the outbreak of World War I to the fall of the Soviet Union. The nomenclature is pertinent for our topic that was dominated by a certain set of assumptions growing from Barth. The exclusion practiced by what became the Biblical Theology Movement is easy to spot in retrospect. On the positivism related to the enterprise, see Burke O. Long, *Planting and Reaping Albright: Politics, Ideology, and Interpreting the Bible* (University Park: Pennsylvania State Univ. Press, 1997).

10. See especially Brevard S. Childs, *Biblical Theology in Crisis* (Philadelphia: Westminster, 1970), and James Barr, "Revelation Through History in the Old Testament and in Modern Theology," *Interp* 17 (1963) 193–205; "The Old Testament and the New Crisis of Biblical Authority," *Interp* 25 (1971) 24–40; *The Bible in the Modern World* (London: SCM, 1973); and *Holy Scripture: Canon, Authority, and Criticism* (Philadelphia: Westminster, 1983). In addition it is important to mention Langdon Gilkey, "Cosmology, Ontology, and the Travail of Biblical Language," *JR* 41 (1961) 194–205.

11. See Walter Brueggemann, "The Loss and Recovery of Creation in Old Testament Theology," *Theology Today* 53 (1996) 177–90, and the references there to Frank Moore Cross, Claus Westermann, and Hans Heinrich Schmid.

12. I have no special concern for the label "postmodern," except that it is a convenient way to reference the quite new interpretive context in which we are now placed. See Walter Brueggemann, *Texts under Negotiation: The Bible and Postmodern Imagination* (Minneapolis: Fortress Press, 1993). For a vigorous and important resistance to postmodernity, see Francis Watson, *Text and Truth: Redefining Biblical Theology* (Grand Rapids: Eerdmans, 1997).

13. For an insistence upon a unified reading that resists pluralism in faithful reading, see Francis Watson, *Text and Truth,* and his earlier book, *Text, Church, and World* (Grand Rapids: Eerdmans, 1994).

14. It seems evident that long-standing theological *hegemony* turns out to be ideological advocacy as does *skepticism* that assumes the ideological

claims of Enlightenment rationality. None is immune from an ideological insistence, so that we must work midst our competing ideological advocacies.

15. On the constitutive power of public speech, see Walter Brueggemann, *Israel's Praise: Doxology against Idolatry and Ideology* (Philadelphia: Fortress Press, 1988) 1–28. A more rigorous discussion than mine would appeal to the work of Foucault.

16. George Steiner, "A Preface to the Hebrew Bible," in *No Passion Spent: Essays 1978–1995* (New Haven: Yale University Press, 1996) 40–87, luminously makes the case for the ways in which the discourse of the Bible is originary. See also Wesley A. Kort, *"Take, Read": Scripture, Textuality, and Cultural Practice* (University Park: Pennsylvania State University Press, 1996).

17. See Jon D. Levenson, "Why Jews Are Not Interested in Biblical Theology," in *The Hebrew Bible, the Old Testament, and Historical Criticism* (Louisville: Westminster John Knox, 1993) 33–61.

18. For what follows, my more extended assessment is given in *Theology of the Old Testament: Testimony, Dispute, Advocacy* (Minneapolis: Fortress Press, 1997).

19. See James A. Sanders, "Adaptable for Life: The Nature and Function of Canon," in *Magnalia Dei: The Mighty Acts of God: Essays on the Bible and Archaeology in Memory of G. Ernest Wright,* ed. Frank Moore Cross, et al. (Garden City, N.Y.: Doubleday, 1976) 531–60.

20. On "testimony" as the decisive genre for biblical theology, see Brueggemann, *Theology of the Old Testament,* 117–44.

21. It is especially Brevard Childs who has insisted that when the text is studied as "scripture," as the holy book of the ecclesial community, the shape and claims of canon are decisive for interpretation. Childs has rightly linked "scripture" to theological intentionality of a quite specific kind. But whereas Childs's notion of Scripture tends to be stable and consolidating, Wesley Kort's *Take, Read* offers a much more radical, lively, and serious notion of the reading of Scripture.

22. On the defining dimension of violence in the text that is assigned to God, see David R. Blumenthal, *Facing the Abusing God: A Theology of Protest* (Louisville: Westminster John Knox, 1993), and Regina M. Schwartz, *The Curse of Cain: The Violent Legacy of Monotheism* (Chicago: Univ. of Chicago Press, 1997).

23. It was of course Barth who focused on the "Wholly Other." The notion of *alterity* has been more fully and helpfully developed in Jewish interpretation, stemming from Martin Buber and given classic formulation by Emmanuel Levinas, *Totality and Infinity: An Essay on Exteriority* (Pittsburgh: Duquesne Univ. Press, 1969). See also George Steiner, *Real Presences* (Chicago: Univ. of Chicago Press, 1989).

24. On the problematic of God's name, see the representative, rather conventional discussion in the essays in *Our Naming of God: Problems and*

Prospects of God-Talk Today, ed. Carl E. Braaten (Minneapolis: Fortress Press, 1989). Kort, *Take, Read,* 133–38, has important suggestions about the *scriptural* deconstruction of patriarchy that dominates Scripture.

25. See Brian Wren, *What Language Shall I Borrow? God-Talk in Worship: A Male Response to Feminist Theology* (New York: Crossroad, 1989), especially chapter 6.

26. As is often remarked, it is important that the name of YHWH is withheld in the long poetic exchange of the book of Job until chapter 38. Such a withholding is surely intentional and strategic for the book of Job.

27. On the witnesses and counter-witnesses, see Walter Brueggemann, "Life-Or-Death, De-Privileged Communication," chapter 2 above.

28. Skepticism is not particularly high ground in intellectual activity. It simply advocates Enlightenment rationality, an increasingly doubtful stance for interpretation. See, for example, the odd use of the term "disinterested" by Philip R. Davies, *Whose Bible is it Anyway?* (JSOTSup 204; Sheffield: Sheffield Academic Press, 1995) 1.

29. On this characterization of postmodernity, see Jean-François Lyotard, *The Postmodern Condition: A Report on Knowledge* (Minneapolis: Univ. of Minnesota Press, 1984).

30. On such a characterization of God, see Dale Patrick, *The Rendering of God in the Old Testament* (OBT; Philadelphia: Fortress Press, 1981).

31. To *imagine alternatively* seems to me a fair notion of what biblical theology is about. Brevard Childs is frequently worried that my emphasis on imagination is to assign too much to human initiative. It is surely the case, however, that any fruitful, faithful interpretation is indeed an act of imagination. See Johanna W. H. van Wijk-Bos, *Reimagining God: The Case for Scriptural Diversity* (Louisville: Westminster John Knox, 1995); Ellen F. Davis, *Imagination Shaped: Old Testament Preaching in the Anglican Tradition* (Valley Forge: Trinity Press International, 1995); and Garret Green, *Imaging God: Theology and the Religious Imagination* (San Francisco: Harper and Row, 1989). And even such a conservative perspective as that of Watson, *Text and Truth,* 325, yields the verdict:

> At the very least, the interpretive tradition that is here in process of formation is an expression of a *creative theological imagination* that has learned to see the scriptural texts in the light of Christ, and Christ in the light of the scriptural texts. (emphasis added)

One must of course make differentiations, but to resist imagination in principle is impossible.

32. The subtitle of Jürgen Moltmann, *The Crucified God,* trans. R. A. Wilson and John Bowden (Minneapolis: Fortress Press, 1993), is "The Cross of Christ as the Foundation and Criticism of Christian Theology."

33. David Tracy, *The Analogical Imagination: Christian Theology and the Culture of Pluralism* (New York: Crossroad, 1981) 3–46.

34. I am aware that by the "Public of the Academy" Tracy refers to the entire university community. Here, because of my particular topic, I refer more explicitly to the guild of Old Testament studies.

35. I take "historical" here broadly to include more recent developments of "social scientific" methods.

36. On the limits and inadequacy of positivistic history for our purposes, see Yosef Hayim Yerushalmi, *Zakhor: Jewish History and Jewish Memory* (Seattle: Univ. of Washington Press, 1982). Said another way, what concerns Old Testament theology must to some extent be concerned with an "emic" approach to the text in distinction from a more conventional "etic" approach. On the distinction, see briefly, Norman K. Gottwald, *The Tribes of Yahweh: A Sociology of the Religion of Liberated Israel, 1250–1050 B.C.E.* (Maryknoll, N.Y.: Orbis, 1979) 785 n. 558.

37. By speaking of such communities in the plural, I refer to both synagogue and church. It is evident that my way of speaking concerns the church, but by the same token, the same issues pertain to the synagogue.

38. This large and important point is well urged by George M. Marsden, *The Soul of the American University: From Protestant Establishment to Established Non-Belief* (Oxford: Oxford Univ. Press, 1994).

39. The interplay of Jews and Christians concerning Scripture is as important as it is vexed. The problematic is already reflected in the different nomenclature for the texts, names that bespeak important issues. See *Hebrew Bible or Old Testament? Studying the Bible in Judaism and Christianity*, ed. Roger Brooks and John J. Collins (Notre Dame: Univ. of Notre Dame Press, 1990).

40. Brevard S. Childs, *Biblical Theology of the Old and New Testaments: Theological Reflection on the Christian Bible* (Minneapolis: Fortress Press, 1992). Clearly Watson, *Text and Truth*, agrees with Childs on this point. See Watson, 209–19, for a reflection upon the work of Childs.

41. Jon D. Levenson, *The Hebrew Bible, the Old Testament, and Historical Criticism*, 80–81 and *passim*. Levenson concludes, "There is no non-particularistic access to these larger contexts" (80).

42. See R. Kendall Soulen, *The God of Israel and Christian Theology* (Minneapolis: Fortress Press, 1996).

43. Fredrick C. Holmgren, *The Old Testament and the Significance of Jesus: Embracing Change—Maintaining Christian Identity: The Emerging Center in Biblical Scholarship* (Grand Rapids: Eerdmans, 1999) has shown how the communities of Judaism, Christianity, and Qumran all engaged in the same "creative/depth" interpretation of scriptural texts.

44. Clearly, to move from the normative text to any of the emergent texts requires an immense act of imagination—surely imagination that is informed by the canonical community. On this kind of freedom and discipline in interpretation, see Charles L. Campbell, *Preaching Jesus: New Directions for Homiletics in Hans Frei's Postliberal Theology* (Grand Rapids: Eerdmans, 1997).

45. The phrase "money government" is from Charles A. Reich, *Opposing the System* (New York: Crown, 1995). See also Herman F. Daly and John B. Cobb Jr., *For the Common Good: Redirecting the Economy toward Community, the Environment, and a Sustainable Future* (Boston: Beacon, 1994); William Greider, *One World: Ready or Not* (New York: S & S Trade, 1997); and Robert Kuttner, *Everything for Sale* (New York: Knopf, 1997).

46. Robert N. Bellah et. al., *Habits of the Heart: Individualism and Commitment in American Life* (Berkeley: Univ. of California Press, 1985).

47. It is, to be sure, a "second naïveté." See Mark I. Wallace, *The Second Naïveté: Barth, Ricoeur, and the New Yale Theology* (Studies in American Biblical Hermeneutics 6; Macon, Ga.: Mercer Univ. Press, 1990).

Credits

"Preaching as Sub-Version" was originally published in *Theology Today* 55 (1998) 195–212. Used by permission.

"Life-or-Death, De-Privileged Communication" was originally published in *Journal for Preachers* 21.4 (Pentecost, 1998) 22–29. Used by permission.

"Together in the Spirit—Beyond Seductive Quarrels" was originally published in *Theology Today* 56 (1999) 152–63. Used by permission.

"Reading as Wounded and as Haunted" originally appeared in a different form ("Haunting Book—Haunted People") in *Word & World* 11 (1991) 62–68. Used by permission.

"Four Indispensable Conversations among Exiles" was originally published in *The Christian Century* 114 (July 2–9, 1997) 630–32. Used by permission.

"The Liturgy of Abundance, The Myth of Scarcity" was originally published in *The Christian Century* (March 24–31, 1999) 342–47.

"Texts That Linger, Not Yet Overcome" was originally published in *Shall Not the Judge of All the Earth Do What Is Right? Studies on the Nature of God in Tribute to James L. Crenshaw*, ed. David Penchansky and Paul L. Redditt (Winona Lake: Eisenbrauns, 2000) 21–41. Used by permission.

"Crisis-Evoked, Crisis- Resolving Speech" was originally published in *Biblical Theology Bulletin* 24 (1994) 95–105. Used by permission.

"The Role of Old Testament Theology in Old Testament Interpretation" was originally published in *In Search of True Wisdom: Essays in Old Testament Interpretation in Honour of Ronald E. Clements*, ed. Edward Ball (JSOTSup 300; Sheffield: Sheffield Academic Press, 1999) 70–88. Used by permission.

Author Index

Ackroyd, Peter R.   136n18
Albertz, Rainer   128n1
Albrektson, Bertil   131n10
Alter, Robert   134n53
Altieri, Charles   43, 129n9–14
Anderson, Francis I.   135n10
Aristotle   85
Balthasar, Hans Urs von   133n26
Barr, James   87, 114, 139n10
Barth, Karl   xi, 112–15, 125n3,
  127n1, 139n9, 140n23
Barton, John   128n8, 136n13
Batto, Bernard F.   137n28
Bellah, Robert N.   1, 121,
  125n2, 143n46
Berger, Peter L.   41, 128n3n4
Blamey, Kathleen   137n31
Bloom, Harold   43
Blumenthal, David R.   87f,
  128n2, 130n34, 134n43–49,
  140n22
Bowden, John   128n1
Braaten, Carl E.   140n24
Branch, Taylor   40, 128n7
Briggs, Charles A.   36
Brooks, Roger   142n39
Brown, Robert McAfee   126n4
Brueggemann, Walter   vii–x,
  126n11n2, 128n5–6, 129n23,
  130n2, 131n14, 133n26n35,
  136n14n21n24, 137n26n30,
  139n11–12, 140n15, 141n27
Buber, Martin   125n3, 140n23
Buckley, Michael J.   1, 47f,
  125n1, 126n1, 129n25–28
Budick, Sanford   125n5
Buechner, Frederick   66–67,
  130n1–3
Butler, James T.   138n4
Butterfield, Fox   6, 125n8

Calvin, John   35, 132n19
Campbell, Charles L.   134n38,
  142n44
Cassell, Eric J.   135n3
Childs, Brevard S.   86–89, 114,
  120, 132n20–21, 133n25n27,
  134n36–37n39–42n50, 135n2,
  137n29, 139n10, 140n21
Clines, David J. A.   95, 131n5,
  135n11
Cobb, John B., Jr.   143n45
Collins, John J.   135n5, 142n39
Crenshaw, James L.   77, 86, 90,
  130n2, 132n18, 133n35
Cross, Frank Moore   114,
  137n27, 139n11, 140n19
Cuddihy, John Murray   44–45,
  125n5, 129n21
Daly, Herman F.   143n45
Daniel, Perky   133n32
Davies, Philip R.   141n28
Davis, Ellen F.   129n29, 131n5,
  141n31
Day, Peggy L.   136n23
Dinesen, Isak   108f, 138n40–45
Desmond, Adrian   133n23
Donner, Herbert   133n27
Dozeman, Thomas B.   135n7
Edelman, Diana Vikander
  127n8
Eichrodt, Walther   113–14
Eldredge, Laurence   138n3
Emerton, J. A.   133n35
Fackenheim, Emil   55, 129n32
Feuerbach, Ludwig   140n15
Fish, Stanley   133n31n33
Fosdick, Harry Emerson   36
Frank, Arthur W.   20, 127n5
Freedman, David Noel   135n10
Frei, Hans   86, 133n26, 134n38

Scripture Index

4:3	136n15	**MARK**		**1 CORINTHIANS**	
6:1	49	1:15	13	1:25	57
		6:30-44	6		
AMOS		8:1-9	6	**2 CORINTHIANS**	
5:7	136	8:21	6	1:3	51
5:24	136	10	75	8	75
6:4-7	63	10:46-49	8		
6:12	136n16	15:34	78	**PHILIPPIANS**	
				3:10	14
NAHUM		**LUKE**			
1:2-3	135n9	1:52-53	16	**COLOSSIANS**	
		4:18-19	15, 38	1:15-17	16
New Testament		7:22	15		
MATTHEW				**HEBREWS**	
27:46	78	**ACTS**		11:11-12	24
		3:6	17	11:13	41
		3:11-16	17		
		3:12-16	18